PRECIOUS CARGO

MY YEAR
DRIVING THE KIDS
ON SCHOOL BUS 3077

CRAIG DAVIDSON

ALFRED A. KNOPF CANADA

PUBLISHED BY ALFRED A. KNOPF CANADA

Copyright © 2016 Craig Davidson

All rights reserved under International and Pan-American Copyright Conventions. No part of this book may be reproduced in any form or by any electronic or mechanical means, including information storage and retrieval systems, without permission in writing from the publisher, except by a reviewer, who may quote brief passages in a review. Published in 2016 by Alfred A. Knopf Canada, a division of Penguin Random House Canada Limited. Distributed in Canada by Penguin Random House Canada Limited, Toronto.

www.penguinrandomhouse.ca

Alfred A. Knopf Canada and colophon are registered trademarks.

Library and Archives Canada Cataloguing in Publication

Davidson, Craig, 1976– , author
Precious cargo : my year driving the kids on school bus 3077 /
Craig Davidson.

Issued in print and electronic formats.

ISBN 978-0-345-81051-9
eBook ISBN 978-0-345-81053-3

1. Davidson, Craig, 1976– . 2. Bus drivers—Canada—Biography.
3. Authors, Canadian (English)—Biography. 4. Students with disabilities—
Transportation. 5. Children with disabilities—Transportation. 6. Children
with disabilities—Care. 7. School buses. I. Title.

LB2864.2.D38 2016   371.9   C2015-905915-1

Book design by Five Seventeen

Cover images: (wall) © Stacey Newman / istockphoto.com;
(man) © Stefanie Grewel / Getty Images; (sky) © tanakawho / flickr
Interior photographs courtesy of the author
Illustration "The Seekers" copyright © 2016 Adam Gorham

Printed and bound in the United States of America

4 6 8 9 7 5

Penguin
Random House
KNOPF CANADA

To the riders on route 3077: The Gang.

—

We are all children of eggs.

ASHANTI PROVERB

When I took the job that led to the book you're holding, I had no intention of writing about it. If anything, I thought maybe I would use a few of my experiences as fodder for a novel, as we writers are notorious for doing. I took a job driving a school bus because I was penniless; it was that simple. But it didn't take me long to realize something special was happening. As a writer, my instinct was to share that with others. So I sent letters to the kids' parents to inform them of my intentions; and I let the kids know that, in addition to being their bus driver, I was a writer—and that someday, maybe, I'd like to write about all of us. I began to take notes, jotting down conversations and my own thoughts during what would turn out to be a transformative year.

When the school year ended I sat down with what I had. I wasn't sure what to do with it. In one sense it was all too raw—the material itself, and my inkling of how to approach it.

There were elements of a personal memoir, but as I saw it, the primary focus should be on those kids who had given me so much joy and opened up my world. These ideas marinated in some cubbyhole of my cortex as I moved on to other work.

Three years after my last day on the job, I decided to write a magazine article. I'd written biggish pieces before—five thousand words or longer, big by magazine standards—and felt this was the best approach. I did a lot of research. I interviewed specialists. The finished piece was roughly seven thousand words, or about one-tenth of the book before you. I was pleased with it, but also felt I'd left much unsaid. In 2013, I sat down to write the entire story. By then, my own life was significantly different. I was a new father, and my bus driving experience had taken on a different resonance in light of this. This book reflects that deepening of experience, or at least I hope it does.

One last note: nearly all the names of people in this book—including the names of all the kids save one—have been changed. In some cases their defining physical characteristics have been altered as well. The kids are adults now, and their names aren't of vital significance to anyone aside from those who love them. What is important is who they were, and are; and who I was, and became. I hope I have managed to be faithful to the experiences we shared.

— CRAIG DAVIDSON, 2015

ONE MORNING IN TIME

I trudged across a field against a late-September wind that flattened my jacket against my chest. The moon was still visible in the early morning sky. The odd vehicle wended down the road bordering the field, pickups mostly. The western foothills rode the earth's curve like the backs of breaching whales. Weak ripples of sunlight washed over the hills to touch blades of wet grass, and in that instant I felt as if I was walking through a field lit up in flame.

The wind died down by the time I reached my bus. My key slid crisply into the lock. I grabbed the Maglite from the cup holder and popped the hood release. Outside, I swept the flashlight beam through the engine compartment. Everything looked tickety-boo.

I shut the hood and stepped inside the bus. The motion-sensor alarm sounded, a staccato *beep-beep-beep*. I keyed the ignition and waited for the glow plugs to warm. The engine fired, coughed, coughed, then caught.

I silenced the alarm. Flicked on the CB radio. Checked my gauges. Got the heaters pumping even though the engine was stone cold. Those small tasks accomplished, I walked between the bench seats with my head tucked so it didn't hit the roof—I'd made the mistake of walking upright my first week on the job, only to have a loose rivet on the roof tear a nifty little groove in my scalp. I pulled the security pin from the rear emergency door and moved back up the aisle, slapping the seatbacks to make sure they were secure. My fingertips brushed against a hardened wad of Windex-coloured gum—the stuff Oliver had been chewing yesterday. We'd be having a little heart-to-heart about gum on the bus, young Master Oliver and I.

I grabbed the broom from under the front seat and walked a circuit around the bus. I took a good swing at each tire to check the inflation, relishing the rubbery *bok* sound. I give the muffler a stiff crack, too. Crouching down, I couldn't see any hoses or wires dangling from the undercarriage. I popped the side door, lowered the wheelchair lift and raised it up again. It had been sticking a bit lately, but today it lifted smoothly. I cracked the emergency door, heard the buzz and shut it. Checked the hazard lights, headlights, high beams, signal lights, fire extinguisher, first aid kit, thermal blankets, traffic triangles. I eyeballed the seven-way mirror system: the fish-eyes, the riot mirror. Checked the windshield wipers and horn and emergency brake, the fan, the squelch button on the CB radio.

Check, check, check, check, check.

All systems go. Rock and roll.

At a quarter to eight I pulled onto the road. The radio murmured: A few Code Yellows; a driver no-show in the north end. The wet streets shone in the new sunlight. I drove past schools and gas stations and a 7-Eleven, rolling with the tide of morning commuters. I pulled up to a stoplight beside a big school bus. The driver and I exchanged the customary school bus driver salute: one hand lifted halfway off the wheel, fingers outspread in casual greeting.

The bus's automatic transmission dropped into second gear as it forged up a hill and slipped effortlessly into third as I crested it. The Rocky Mountains rose into air so blue and clear it held the sparkling effervescence of freshly poured seltzer. I pulled up beside a white-sided house. I angled the front tires into the curb, flicked on the hazards and engaged the parking brake, then hopped out and snugged wooden blocks under the rear tires.

The garage door rattled up. Calvin walked down a wooden ramp that connected the garage's inner door to the driveway. He waved and said, "He'll be out in a minute."

I lowered the wheelchair ramp. Inside the house, through an open door, I could see Jake getting ready. His sister was brushing his hair. His caregiver was attempting, unsuccessfully, to coax him into eating another bite of toast. The door swung shut. When it opened again, Jake drove through the doorway and down the ramp. His wheelchair accelerated at breakneck speed and took a sharp corner poorly—Jake was a bad driver; it was something he'd freely admit. The front tires clipped the garage wall.

"Oi!" Calvin called after him. "Careful, my son!"

"Craig!" the boy shouted, his face lit like a supernova. "You are never going to *believe* what happened!"

I smiled. Not because I wouldn't believe what he was about to tell me—most often, what he had to say was entirely reasonable, sometimes even mundane. I smiled because his enthusiasm kindled a giddiness in me: a soda-pop fizz that started in my belly and percolated all through me.

"So what's this amazing news?" I asked.

The boy cast a glance over his shoulder at his father. His voice dropped to a conspiratorial whisper.

"Tell you later."

Ah. So it was to be a bus story. The bus was the confessional, the cone of silence, the chamber of shared confidences. After I got Jake on board, his wheelchair strapped down and his chest buckled in safely, he would tell me. He always did.

The exact words he would use, in fact, would be—

Ah, but we're getting ahead of ourselves.

There's a story I should tell you before we get to this one—before Jake and Oliver and Vincent and Gavin and Nadja. Before bus 3077 and route 412. Before my stories and those kids' stories became meshed.

SUMMER

"THE SEEKERS,"
an unpublished novel

My name is Bloodhound. That's not my real name. It was the name I was given when my new life began.

I am the last of the Seekers. There were five of us. Goshawk. Panther. Kodiak. Lamprey.

And me. Bloodhound.

I miss the others. You're supposed to miss your friends, right? I even miss the one who wasn't entirely real. He was real enough to me—and as someone I love once said: reality is highly overrated.

How long has it been since I saw them last? Feels like forever. But time gets weird when you don't experience it the way a human being is supposed to—in a straight line. It's hard when you've skipped around the time-stream, meeting the same people at different points in their lives, decades apart. Live that way long enough and your own history gets so broken up you can't make heads or tails of it. Your own chronology fractures like jagged shards of a mirror that you can't piece back together.

Where does time go? I've asked this often. And of course time doesn't "go" anywhere. So why do we often sense it as something we try to catch but can't, like trying to snare a darting minnow with your bare hands? I guess I should know the answer better than anyone. I've experienced more pure time than any other living creature has or ever will. But I still don't know where it goes. I only know it's gone. It has taken everything with it. My friends and what we shared. All swallowed up in time.

But I am still here. The Bloodhound. Last of the Seekers.

I slipped through time.

I lived through generations.

I hunted gods.

1.

The school principal was tall and broad across the shoulders. His grey-flecked hair tumbled past his collarbones. He wore a bolo tie set off by a blue topaz.

It was July of 2008, and I had arrived for my interview lathered in sweat. My car's radiator fan was busted and I couldn't afford to get it repaired. The only way to stop the rad from overheating was to blast the excess hot air through the vents into my face. A crucifix of sweat darkened the front of my dress shirt even as the school's a/c raised gooseflesh on my forearms.

I'd applied for the position of Lunch Supervisor. I was thirty-two years old. I had prior experience with both lunch, as a consumer of it, and supervision, from an amusement park job where someone had slapped a badge on my chest and paid me an extra quarter an hour, but I had no specific experience in Lunch Supervision *per se*. According to the job description, the successful applicant would, among other duties, clean up the food prep area following procedures outlined in the Food Services Handbook. I had no specific experience in this either, though I'd washed my fair share of dishes.

What *was* my background? A variety of odd jobs: tree planter, whale watcher, ESL teacher, house painter, librarian. Prone to wanderlust, I had never worked any job for long. I'd cobbled together one of those whimsical CVs you often read in writers' biographies: *Before taking up writing full-time, Writer X toiled as an itinerant shepherd, a cook at a nudist camp, an apprentice embalmer, an [insert bizarre short-term gig].* Those bios were fun to read on the back flap of a book, but when one of them crossed the desk of a fellow such as this principal . . . you couldn't blame him for suspecting he was dealing with a flake. A sweaty flake.

The sweat was one part broken radiator and two parts desperation. I *needed* this job. I had reached a point in my life where I had begun to apply for gigs willy-nilly, as the ones I may have once competently vied for had been snatched up by more qualified applicants. My bank account—never robust—had dwindled to the point where, upon spying the balance, you might think it belonged to a boy who had cleared a few bucks mowing his neighbours' lawns. I had begun to look for jobs whose requirements entailed, basically, a pulse. And even then I was coming up empty handed. The week prior I'd applied to be a worm harvester. As I interpreted it, the role of a harvester was to comb through enormous tubs of dirt, plucking up nightcrawlers for sale at bait shops and the like. The supervisor of the worm-harvesting operation had one critical need: that I own rubber boots. I wasn't wearing any during the interview but assured him I could get a pair. The supervisor seemed dubious—less of my ability to acquire boots, I assumed, than his sense that I did not have the harvester's *je ne sais quoi*, me with my pillowy hands and overeducated face. He sent me away. A few steps outside his office the realization dawned: *Craig Davidson, you are not worm-harvester material.*

"What drew you to this opportunity?" the principal now asked.

My crippling poverty? I thought but did not say.

"Well, let's see. I get along well with kids." I smiled and tried a joke: "Plus I'm a huge fan of tater tots."

The principal gave me the kind of look I imagined he might make if he were to spy a slug in his slipper. What had he expected me to say—that as a teen I'd been the Dishwashing King of Crystal Lake Camp and was itching to get back into my old championship form? He rose and cracked the window. I could hear a custodian banging away on the playground equipment, fixing something; each hammer stroke rang crisply in the afternoon air. The principal ran his eyes over my resume again.

"You worked at a library in your last job. Not for very long by the looks of it."

"It's an interesting story," I said, though I could tell he would not find it remotely interesting. "We had a ficus plant behind the checkout desk. I watered it. There was a plastic watering can right beside it. Anyway, turns out it was another librarian's job. We all had our little assigned tasks. One was to order golf pencils. Another was to mix juice for storytime. So I watered this plant and it was someone else's job and that person got ticked and reported me. My supervisor reprimanded me for stepping outside of my bounds and it all felt so stifling and suffocating that I . . . in a rash moment I . . . well, I quit."

He eyed me evenly. "You quit. Over a ficus."

No, I didn't quit over a ficus—not *exactly*. The whole ficus fandango drove me over the edge. I could have told him I was standing up to a bureaucratic system that doled out demerits for watering plants, but who cared? The library had already hired somebody else to check the books out. Somebody who obeyed the rules and wasn't a brash firebrand—who buckled down and ordered the goddamn golf pencils, as the task-board clearly stated. So why *had* I watered that plant? To make an unnecessary and half-assed point. *Well, bully for you, Karen Silkwood!* Trying to defend myself now would make me look more impulsive, more prone to pique, more . . . flaky. It would only convince the principal that I was liable to quit this job for no good reason, too.

The truth was, I'd quit the library while riding a minor high. I had sold a piece of writing to a big American magazine.

Davidson was on the comeback trail! Find some other stiff to order your golf pencils, I'd crowed inwardly. Stupid, stupid me.

The principal flipped my application facedown on his desk and pinned it under his thumb.

"I want to thank you for coming in."

I exited the school doors under a metallic sky. Walking back to my car in the crucible of that late summer afternoon, one undeniable fact struck me like a wrecking ball.

Craig Davidson, you are not Lunch Supervisor material.

I started the car. Pebbles of safety glass sparkled on the floormats. Just last week, punks had smashed the driver's side window to steal the spare change from the cup-holder. I could have used those coins—probably more than those faceless punks did. I drove home beneath scalloped clouds, the day's swelter made worse by the broiled air pouring from the vents. On the upside, the busted window that I could not afford to fix allowed a semi-cooling zephyr to blow across my face. I knuckled sweat from my eyes and thumped the steering wheel.

"Davidson, you dingbat. You blew it."

At home I put the kettle on and ripped open a few packets of No Name Instant Oatmeal. The stuff was cheap. It filled you up. As a university student I'd lived for weeks on potatoes. A ten-pound bag of spuds ran you four bucks. Baked, boiled, mashed. That had been nearly fifteen years ago, and I'd never thought I might be back on the potato diet. But it was looming.

The kettle shrieked. I doused the oatmeal and ate with determined bites. Yum, yum, yum. A bumblebee fretted behind the kitchen drapes. The same one, I was sure, that had flown through the unscreened window every day for the past week. It must have left a pheromone trail, thinking there was something tasty in my kitchen. Poor misguided thing.

I covered the bee with a glass and slid a sheet of paper underneath. The bee buzzed hectically, the paper vibrating against my fingers. I took it to the front door and let it fly away. See you tomorrow, little guy!

A sheet of Xeroxed paper was poking out of the mailbox.

Immediate openings for School Bus Drivers! it read.

No experience necessary!

Interesting, interesting.

Will provide quality training!

Well, assumedly.

Must pass background check and drug screening.

No skeletons of that sort rattling around in my closet.

It was your textbook case of mutual desperation: A company eager enough to solicit applicants through leaflet bombing meets a man in dire enough straits to make life-altering decisions based on random papers shoved into his mailbox. There was a number. I called it. When nobody picked up I left a message. Before long a female recruiter called back.

"You left a message?"

"I did."

"You did!"

She seemed somehow relieved to hear it. An interview was scheduled for the very next day.

2.

The question you might be asking, dear reader, is: *Craig, how had your existence become so dismal?* I was youngish, educated, with no criminal record and in full control of my faculties. What exactly was my problem?

Let's go back—*aaaaaaall* the way back, to childhood.

I've always liked to tell stories. I say *liked*, but at first it was a matter of social necessity. As early as elementary school most of us start to get a sense of what in our bodies and intellects sets us apart—or more importantly, marks us as part of a group. The process starts with what you *aren't*; you cross off possibilities until you discover what you *are*, what camp you belong to. As a rotund, orange-haired, awkward and non-athletic kid, "brooding cool cat" and "future Olympian" were quickly crossed off my list. In music class I was given the triangle and still managed to muff my part in the recital, so "musical prodigy" was right out. Ditto "tough guy." It came down to the dregs: "withdrawn bookworm," "future inmate," "kid who eats his own scabs." Which left only one vector for a boy like me: class clown.

To this, I was perfectly suited. There's something innately funny about chubby, schlumphy guys. I had an unhinged physicality that made every pratfall funnier, but also, like many fat kids, my personality held a benign harmlessness. And as with most class clowns, the divide between laughing *with* you and laughing *at* you was murky: that people were *laughing* at all was my primary concern.

During those formative years, making my classmates howl was my only social currency. I was nothing without those laughs, and like an addict I'd do anything to get them. Lowest-common-denominator stuff worked best: I'd pretend to trip over the bike rack, or choke myself with my own hand coming up through the collar of my shirt (a trick one of my uncles had taught me, no doubt sensing I'd need it to survive). If those tricks failed, I'd cause some minor disruption in class. My teachers were forbearing to a fault; I'm sure they recognized my desperate attempt to avoid being relegated to the nether reaches of the schoolyard where the scab-eaters and other pariahs wandered like lonely ghosts. Sometimes I'd go too far and would be exiled to the hallway. I was secretly grateful: nobody expected me to be funny in the hall. I could just sit quietly and get some work done. But then the teacher would let me in, and I was like a comedian pulled back onstage for an encore. I'd have to whip out the dog-and-pony again.

As the years went on I spent more and more time in the hall.

My years as a clown shaped me in three ways. First, they made me realize that I enjoy performing and making people laugh—making people *happy*. It's an elemental joy, making another person laugh. It got so that my classmates were laughing before I did anything; a comedic possibility would pop up and heads would swivel in my direction and in that silence lurked an unspoken expectation: *Oh, now Davidson's gonna do something to crack us up.*

Second, those years gave me a sense of narrative. I learned how to tell a story. There is the anatomy of a story in most jokes: you're establishing story beats and expectations, maybe building in a callback that will bring the whole class down. Of course I wasn't aware of these formal terms back then. I was just cracking wise. But I'm sure many creative types look back at their childhoods and discover that their talents—often built of necessity, just to find a place for themselves—established themselves at that early stage.

Finally, for better or worse, those years established a deep obsessive streak within me. The desire to be *the best* at something, if only in my little pond. Every so often someone would try to snatch away my clown crown. Who can forget the epic battle between Paul Carley and me in Grade 8, when I trumped him with my devastating puppet show in drama class? (Drama class, as all reformed class clowns know, is like methadone for our breed). Or the wearying war of attrition between me and Ken Pope, a battle that raged through

Grade 10 and ended in an uneasy detente? The answer is: precisely *one* person remembers. Paul and Ken have long forgotten, I'm sure. But it mattered like hell to me.

By my early twenties I was an obsessional mind in search of its pole star. But by then a trace of skepticism had crept into me. The world was no longer the mostly happy place it had been in my youth; I couldn't accept its failings (or my own) uncritically. I'd taken a creative writing class in Grade 12 and the experience of writing felt hand-in-glove. I could perform on the page; no longer would I have to make a fool of myself to enjoy the euphoria from making other people *feel* something. Plus, let's face it: funny guys don't get the girl. Oh, girls will tell you that's not the case—and heck, maybe it's true for other comedians—but no girl had ever told me, *Oh, Craig, take me home and whisper sweet knock-knock jokes in my ear!* Meanwhile, I had noticed many faux-intellectual prats having great success with their berets and acoustic guitars and studiously dog-eared volumes of Proust's *In Search of Lost Time*. So okay, I'd be one of those guys. The moody intellectual, thinker of deep thoughts.

My early to mid-twenties were a lesson in failure, which, if nothing else, prepared me for sundry future catastrophes. Those early failures were of a common sort: my first stories simply weren't very good. My themes were less what I wanted to write about and more what I thought I *ought to* be writing about. Turmoil-laden stories about characters coping with the loss of a child, or airless tales where couples fell ungraciously out of love. Stories I had no entry into, having had none of those experiences. Or I'd write hackneyed rip-offs of Hemingway and Carver, aping a style that seemed disarmingly simple, yet was anything but.

I would print these stories out and put them in envelopes and mail them out *everywhere*, bombing magazines, journals, fledgling online markets. I spent more on paper and ink and postage than I did on food. Then I'd wait and check the mailbox . . . and be rejected. Hundreds of times. I never did anything so self-immolating as fill a pillowcase with my rejection slips, but had I done so I could have laid my head down and had a terrible night's sleep on that crinkly cushion of failure.

My first acceptance was at a website that ran three stories *a day*. They paid zilch. But when that email came in telling me that something I'd written would be published—no, not even: *posted*—I felt an elation unequalled by anything I'd so far experienced in my adult life. I did a giddy, awkward dance in my grotty basement apartment, the joy pouring out of me. In some ways my entire career is an attempt to get back to that moment of pure happiness. It's like your first taste of ice cream, your first kiss, your first a lot of things: its pleasures are unmatchable because you have no basis for comparison. But what keeps you coming back—sometimes at great personal expense—is the unsullied memory of that joy. Even if somewhere deep in your heart you know you'll never feel quite that way again.

I got better. There's no trick, no shortcut. Ass in chair. Incrementally, day by day, I became more skillful. And one day I was good enough, in someone's estimation. I sold four stories in the span of a month to markets that had rejected me for years. Boom, boom, boom, boom. The floodgates opened. All the work I'd put in, all the rejection and failure and bucking up and trying again, it bore fruit. I got an agent. She handed my collection of stories to an editor at some glitzy cocktail party. He read it quickly and called her with a proposal: he'd make an offer on the collection, plus a novel to come. We took the deal. We'd have been fools not to.

It happened overnight. You hear that sometimes, don't you? It didn't, of course. Not for me, anyway. That editor's offer was the result of years of hard work. But it did feel as if I was suddenly on a different trajectory. No longer did I have to toil at odd jobs to stay afloat, writing in every spare moment. The book deal was enough to survive on for a year and a half, maybe two if I scrimped.

I was living in Calgary by that time. I walked to a liquor store and bought a bottle of modestly priced scotch, which seemed a fine and celebratory quaff. I came home and phoned my parents. Huzzahs, huzzahs all around! Then I hung up and drank a glass of scotch. At twenty-eight, I was a full-time writer.

That was my mistake—and it was the result of simple ignorance. My father was a banker. My mother was a nurse. They had been in these professions their entire working lives.

It had taken me a little longer to establish myself, but now I figured I'd write books until I was rich enough to do something else or got hit by a speeding bus or hit sixty-five and quit. I assumed my future was secure. But that's not how it works.

My first book, a collection of stories, came out in 2005. In the most pragmatic sense, it did exactly what it was supposed to do—that is, establish me as "a promising young writer to watch." Everything after that hinged on the novel to follow. It almost always does.

Ah, that novel. Looking back, I'm not sure if it is a good book or not. The thing I do know is that it wasn't good enough. Maybe expectations—mine, those of my publishers—were unreasonably high. Or maybe they were appropriately high and I simply failed to meet them. After reading the manuscript, my then-agent called and described it with the following analogy:

"Craig, I think I understand how *you* see what you've written. If the book is a car, then you saw yourself sitting behind the wheel and driving it however many chapters, let's say twenty chapters, getting to your destination and thinking, *Okay, good trip.* I see it differently. I see that car as travelling three or four chapters then flying through the guardrail off a cliff, where it continued to burn for the next sixteen or so chapters. That's how I see it. I'm sorry."

She wasn't sorry, but then her job wasn't to be sorry. Her job was to try to stop me from making career-crippling mistakes. Plus, she was right. A month later my American editor read the manuscript and promptly dropped the whole book. This was nearly unheard of. The publisher was still on the hook to pay my advance. My agent assured me of this, as if I should be happy they were honouring their commitment. The way I saw it was different: they paid for the right to *not* publish my book. For cash-strapped publishers, this was a drastic step.

I remember when that call came through. I was living in a shoebox attic apartment in Iowa City. I had been repairing my eyeglasses; a tiny screw had come loose from the nosepiece. As my agent talked I nodded numbly, saying, "Uh-huh . . . uh-huh . . . okay." I hung up. The little screw had rolled off the desk into the threadbare carpet. I got down on my knees. Things felt better on the floor. I curled into a fetal ball. And then I looked for that damn screw for *hours*. My mind kept sprinting towards the reality of what that phone call meant— my dreams, my sense of what my future was supposed to hold, draining through my fingers—and retreating back to the task of locating that screw. I was talking to myself, repeating things I should have said on the phone, things I should have done differently with the book, then grinding my teeth and forcing myself to look for that stupid damn screw. I never did find it.

The novel came out in Canada in the fall of 2007. I held out a slim hope that everyone was wrong. My agent was a young woman. My American editor had been an older man. The book wasn't written for them. It was for guys like me: twenty-something dudes who were diffusely angry at the world and didn't understand the unsatisfying path their lives had taken.

Evidently those dudes don't read—or anyway, they didn't read my novel.

And so, nearly as fast as it had happened, my career was over. A fleeting rise followed by a swift and shocking fall. I became persona non grata. Nobody wanted to be in the Craig Davidson business, for good reason. I parted ways with my agent. The money, never significant, dried up.

In retrospect, I wasn't much fun to be around during this time. Argumentative, mopey, brittle: I became a different person. I was aware of this, too, but it was hard to root myself out of my funk. I nursed the terrible thought that I may have thrown away the only shot I'd ever have at the career—the *life*—I wanted. After all those years of rejection, the self-imposed isolation, the dreaming and hoping and *wanting* so damn badly. It seemed unfair. Shouldn't the best and most productive years lie ahead of me? Worst of all was the knowledge that I'd done this to myself.

———

Let me pause and take a step back here. Honestly, things weren't *that* bad. I know I was fantastically lucky in so many regards. And I am archly aware of the usual trappings of books such as this one. Their storylines often involve the death of a loved one, a divorce, rehab and recovery, crummy parents, a history of abuse. My own narrative has none of that. Nobody had died. Seeing as no one had ever expressed the remotest interest in marrying me, I hadn't been divorced. My childhood was great, my parents loving and supportive. I had my health.

Simply put, I was a failure. It's the most commonplace kind of heartbreak to befall any of us, right? If you're relatively young, perhaps the pain's a bit sharper. Failing at seventy is one matter. But to fail cataclysmically at thirty? You're staring down the barrel of the rest of your life—fifty, sixty years if you're especially hale: a minor infinity for that failure to sink inside your bones and grind you down.

Failure affected me in the common ways. I drank too much. Money was scarce but there was always enough for an afternoon six-pack. I drank the heart out of many a fine afternoon. I had trouble sleeping. When I did, my dreams were weird. Dreams where burly loan sharks extorted pitiful sums of money from me—and when I pulled my pockets out to show them I had nothing, moths would fly up like in a Depression-era cartoon strip. I had a recurrent dream where a stunningly beautiful woman stole my mail: I'd watch her do it through my kitchen window, a woman in a black evening dress picking through my bills and flyers while staring back at me with casual scorn. My insomnia was so intense that I'd be up at four o'clock in the morning, alone in the pin-eyed darkness, watching taped Canadian parliamentary sessions on TV. A bunch of buffoons—the duly elected leaders of our great land—shouting each other down and pounding their chests like incensed gorillas. I found a brand of over-the-counter sleeping pills that worked for a while until I developed a tolerance. I discovered that, in time, you develop a tolerance for just about everything.

I was back to working menial, no-brainer jobs to stay afloat. I didn't write for months. I treaded water, hoping something would happen—maybe the phone would ring, a conference call with my old editors on the line: *Craig, we were fools! We want you back!*

I marvelled at how *ordinary* my existence had become. I'd never wanted a normal life. I yearned for something magical, bigger than myself. The life of a writer. A life of the mind. One where I made my own hours and went on book tours. *That Davidson!* I imagined people saying. *How clever! How profound!* Ordinariness was anathema—a living death. If I had wanted to be ordinary I would have returned to my home-town and filled sacks of sugar or drilled out ignition collars in one of a half-dozen factories; I would have stared across the conveyor belt ferrying granola bars or brake pads, spotting the guys I'd gone to high school with, our faces florid and basset-houndy. On the weekends we'd drive four-wheelers to get away from the wives we'd married too early and the kids we could barely comprehend, then drink Black Label and watch the hockey game without speaking. Any walking dick could get that. And yet, there I was. Seeking an exceptional life, I'd achieved a thuddingly ordinary one.

I spent days sunk in self-pity. *Why me?* If you worked hard and sacrificed, you should succeed. Isn't that what our parents told us? Then I'd get angry at myself for being so self-centred when there were people who couldn't walk, who had lost limbs, whose entire families had been washed away in tsunamis or buried in earthquakes. Other times I couldn't even rally myself to give a damn. *Meh,* I'd think. *Who cares? So I suck. Life will go on. Under a reduced ceiling, but whatever. I officially join the ranks of the failed. It's a big club; I can get lost among its membership, blending in with the other schlubs and no-hopers.*

Sometimes, though, I cared a whole lot. Failure carries a weight. Nobody tells you this. Cinderblocks stacked on your chest and piled atop your skull; you develop a persistent slump, your shoulders rounded in defeat. People can sense it. They avoid you as if you've got scabies. That's a wise decision. Being in the company of a failure isn't pleasant. There's a terrible desire amongst failures to pull someone else into their pit of despair so they can have some company while they wallow.

And loneliness. Never had I felt it quite so keenly. I could stomach being alone; this was partly the reason I took to writing: when you're alone, you don't feel the need to perform for anyone. But for most of my twenties I'd put everything into writing—every ounce of energy and time. I'd resolved to take the thimbleful of talent I'd been blessed with and wring a career out of it. I'd bury better writers and leave them in the dirt because I was willing to work harder and take more rejection, to isolate and even wreck myself. I assumed my family and friends understood. *There goes Craig, obsessing away.* I adhered to the ethos articulated by Neil McCauley, Robert De Niro's character in *Heat*: "Don't let yourself get attached to anything you are not willing to walk out on in thirty seconds flat, if you feel the heat around the corner." I had no obligations to anyone, no moorings, nothing to distract me. I had chosen to put the remainder of my life into deep freeze until I was able to view myself as a success. But now I asked: What did that even *mean*? Success—what was its shape? Having more money than I could ever spend? Hitting the bestseller list? Becoming a critical darling? In truth, none of these would have been enough—not for the long haul. The mountain goes up and up, and when you think you've reached the summit, the clouds part to reveal another peak and you have to start climbing again.

The biggest fear was the sense that I'd ripped myself to shreds in pursuit of a goal only to discover that ultimately it wasn't enough. How far short had I fallen? You can never tell, and that—the not knowing—it chews you up. You look inside yourself, find the needle on your internal gas tank and ask: *What the hell is left? Is it enough—and if so, for what? To just get by? Another sixty years of this?*

The loneliness sought out the new emptiness in me and made a home. I saw almost nobody. I went to the gym and worked out ruthlessly, punishing myself. I ran endless miles through the city streets when the rest of the world was sleeping. Friday nights were spent in front of the TV. Saturdays the same. It felt safer that way. I didn't have to be around people who'd known me before the collapse, people who had spent their twenties accumulating those things one naturally does at that time: wives and husbands and homes and careers and families. All those things I'd so foolishly thought I could get for myself, later. If those people were to meet me now, I thought, they would find themselves in the presence of a stranger.

3.

Some people hold an uncharitable view of school bus drivers. In the minds of such people, drivers exist as ample-bottomed, Jordache-jean-clad entities who gather by their buses before the final school bell to exchange photographs of their grandchildren and cats, smoke absurdly long and skinny mentholated cigarettes (or pipes, should they be exceedingly aged or whimsical), and carp about sciatica, lumbago, varicose veins, and ailments of an old-timey nature: brain fog, milk leg, the horrors, wandering bladder, grocer's itch, swamp lung and the 'stinks.

I had never pictured myself amongst their number, at least not at my relatively youthful age. What if I was hired? I envisioned myself smoking those ridiculous mentholated cigs and lamenting the theft of my beaded seat cushion while my fellow bus drivers clucked sympathetically. *Kids these days, eh?* I'd winge. *Scofflaws and hoodlums! Where's the respect gone, that's what I wanna know!* Ah, well. I needed the job. Unfit for the student nourishment sector, surely I could secure a foothold in the student transport field.

The hiring centre was nestled in a hive of industrial lots in the city's north end. I drove past a yard of yellow buses parked nose-to-bumper, tight as sardines in a tin. Rusted emergency doors were stacked like playing cards in one corner of the yard.

The offices resembled a hamster's Habitrail system: some portables were stacked atop one another; others were linked with insulated walkways. Perhaps it was no coincidence that my interviewer had the harried demeanour of someone trapped on a wheel—her legs forever pumping and pumping, never going anyplace.

She handed me a clear plastic cup and pointed me towards the toilets. When I returned, she took it away and performed "tests" on it. When she came back from the lab, it was with lavish and blush-worthy praise for my urine sample.

"It's super-clean," she said jocularly. "Are you a saint or something?"

She leaned in and told me, conspiratorially, that some applicants had been known to cheat on their screening tests. "They get clean urine off the Internet."

Shocking news indeed. Drug-addled wannabe drivers had the disposable income to lavish on pricey Internet urine? So why was I messing around with bus driving when I could make a mint selling my exceptional piss to unemployed druggies? My hopes were dashed when she clarified: these scoundrels did not buy *actual* urine; they bought detox pills to clean out their urinary tracts and thwart the tests.

The interview went well. My every answer elicited an emphatic nod. I began to wonder just how deeply I could manifest signs of runaway psychosis and still pass muster.

INTERVIEWER: You're driving the bus and some rowdy students begin to cause a disturbance. What do you do?

ME: Well, ma'am, I don't cotton to disobedience. So if any of those little turds gives me guff you'd better believe I'd start firing them out the windows like paper airplanes.

INTERVIEWER: You, sir, are a doer. Not a thinker. I admire that.

Of course, I wouldn't have dreamt of answering that way. I needed the job too damn bad. The next day I headed to the doctor's office for a physical exam. The sawbones said I was one of the fittest bus driver applicants he'd seen that year, a compliment that ranked with being the trimmest child at fat camp, but I took it: ego boosts were few and far between back then.

—

Training began in early August. There were eight hopefuls. We were each given a reflective yellow vest with TRAINEE stamped on the back. Our week-long training junket consisted of four hours in class daily, followed by afternoons on the road in a bus. We had a couple of washouts in the first few days. A sunny retiree named Connie said the ergonomics of the bus's seats wreaked havoc on her surgically reconstructed knee. Another guy whose name I never caught showed up two hours late the third morning smelling like he'd been marinating in a bathtub of Rebel Yell whiskey. I assume he was told to turn in his "yellow," as I never saw him again.

Morning sessions were held in a portable in the bus yard. Posters of grinning bus drivers were tacked to the walls alongside the company's slogan: IF YOU CAN'T DO IT SAFELY, DON'T DO IT! Our instructor was a buzz-cut retiree who wore a sweatshirt with a loon stencilled on it.

"I'm not as sharp as I once was," he revealed without prompting. "I don't have Alzheimer's, but I will cop to having *some*timers."

If so, I never noticed. On the contrary: he was sharp as a tack, and a conscientious instructor. He took his duties seriously and his dogged sense of care rubbed off on all of us.

"Remember," he said, "you aren't driving potatoes. You've got living, breathing creatures on board your buses. The legal definition of what you transport is 'precious cargo.'"

We watched a lot of videos produced by the good, if alarmist, folks at the Crisis Prevention Institute. These were produced in grainy VHS and hosted by men sporting acid-wash jeans and push-broom moustaches. I figured the fact that the tapes were dated wasn't worrisome: how many advances could there be in bus driving technology?

One of the videos featured a particularly memorable scene: a manic, possibly method child actor was waving a pistol on a packed bus as his classmates cowered. "I can't *take it* anymore!" the boy screamed. He held the pistol to his woebegone bus driver's head and hissed, "You're scared, aren't you?" The bus driver whimpered, "You bet I'm scared," at which point the prepubescent gun-toter shouted: "You crybaby! And the rest of you, treating me like some kind of *freak!*" The situation was amicably resolved, though I can no longer recall how.

Trainees became well-versed in all manner of assaults one might sustain in the line of service. Punches, kicks, headlocks, wads of spit. We learned that a pinch can be classified as assault "if held for an inappropriate length of time"—prompting me to wonder: What poor soul has to test that threshold?

We were also taught protocols for addressing parents who felt their child was being unfairly treated or teased on the bus. Our instructor told us the unhappy tale of a driver who was decked, stone cold, by an enraged father.

"They don't pay us enough to go through *that*," he said gravely.

A spill kit video instructed us on the techniques for cleaning up vomit and urine, blood and feces—all the colours of the bodily rainbow. Another illustrated the procedure for evacuating a bus that was on fire: I particularly remember the driver fashioning a papoose for wheelchair-bound students out of the on board emergency blankets. Our instructor outlined the triage methodology following a bus crash.

"If a student's skin is ashy-grey or cold," he said, "they may have lost too much blood to survive. In that instance you'd want to move on to the next wounded child."

We sat up straighter, hearing that. Could that *happen?* Having to make those life-and-death decisions? Good Lord, most of us only wanted to make a little folding cash.

By midweek we were watching a video where child-sized crash-test dummies on a conventional seventy-two-seat bus got torn apart on impact, snapped in half against the seat backs or cleaved in two by lap belts. A second video showed a pair of high school students grab-assing in the parking lot after last bell: one of them falls down and, as the bus pulls away, it runs over his legs. This was depicted with chintzy 80s special effects, sure, a couple of empty trouser legs stuffed with styrofoam packing peanuts, but still, the notion of running over a child's legs was chilling. Yet another video illustrated how a young child viewed the world—he or she will heedlessly follow a bouncing ball between two parked cars and onto the road, awareness not yet developed enough to conceive of any threat lurking outside that narrow focus.

"Children see the world in a fundamentally different way," our instructor said. "You can't see it how they do—that's beaten out of us by now. But you have to be prepared for it."

He moved on to a series of photos. The first showed a bus that had stalled on a railway track only to be hit by an onrushing locomotive. The kids had been evacuated by then, thank goodness. Post-collision, the bus looked like a yellow beer can sliced in half. Another photo illustrated the aftermath of a near-collision between a bus and a minivan at a residential four-way stop; the bus had hopped over the curb, crossed someone's lawn, and barrelled through the bay window of a suburban home.

"Clearly, this could have been avoided," our instructor said dryly.

After a quick break to allow us to digest the various calamities that might befall us, our instructor outlined the four "codes" a driver may use over the CB radio.

1. Code Yellow, for mechanical malfunction.
2. Code Red, for a fender-bender or a hit-and-run.
3. Code Blue, for 911 emergency assistance.
4. Code Orange, for a missing child.

"Please, everyone," he stressed. "Check your bus after each run. Last winter a driver left a six-year-old on her bus. She had fallen asleep in the back seat. The child woke up in the bus yard at night, dead of winter, in a locked and empty vehicle."

We were given an hour at noon for lunch. One day I shared a picnic table with a fellow trainee. He had a carbuncled nose and skin the colour of old piano keys. One side of his neck was netted with shallow scratches as if he'd been attacked by a wrathful budgie. He didn't have a lunch, per se. Instead, he was eating packets of Saltine crackers: two crackers per pack, the kind you get at a diner with your soup. His pockets were full of crackers.

"This is shaping up to be better than my last job," he said, bits of half-masticated cracker showering from his lips.

"What was that?" I asked.

"I was in the flyer delivery industry."

The fellow proceeded to pour forth a tale of woe wherein he cast himself as the victim of a pack of evil schoolboys whose flyer routes he'd unsuccessfully tried to usurp.

"I told the flyer kingpin—the guy in charge of doling out the routes, okay?—I told him hey, buddy, I'll get those flyers into mailboxes where they belong. I'm a goer, you understand. I *go*. All day. These kids you got working?" The man lip-farted. "Gimme a break! They'll chuck all your flyers in a dumpster and call it a day!"

I can't say what was more shocking: the fact that a grown man was crowing about trying to steal after-school jobs from children while upholding his unimpeachable decency, or the fact that the flyer distribution industry had kingpins.

"Those boys were vicious little pricks," the man went on. "Sore losers, all of them. They stuck a steak knife in my bike tire."

This odd organism washed out before the end of the week. In all, a good call. He did not appear to actively enjoy the company of kids. But he was an anomaly. My fellow trainees were uniformly upstanding folk.

It's true that I had embarked on the training sessions with a jaundiced view of the fraternity. Female bus drivers were,

I imagined, battleaxes who smoked American Spirits, wore clearance-centre Wranglers, and had forty-year-old sons who drove fourth-hand Camaros. Or they were guys whose bodies appeared to be composed of braided coat-hangers beneath their loose-fitting lumberjack shirts, and whose teeth resembled a freeway pileup of tiny grey sedans. They were folk who spouted dull double-entendres and had spent the past summer picking apples for three bucks a bushel.

I was startled to discover (though I should not have been) that most drivers didn't fit these, or any, stereotypes. They were young single mothers, university students, doting grandmothers, new immigrants, and people like me who tumbled into the opportunity ass-backwards. Everyone was seeking to do something valuable for a few hours a day. They were good, smart, caring people who took their job seriously and did it well.

———

Afternoons were spent on the road. My trainer's name was Don. He was stocky and square-shouldered, his black hair combed back from his forehead and greying slightly around the ears. He wore spectacles with a pair of clip-on sunglasses fastened to the nosepiece. His cherubic face was married to a powerful, utilitarian body. Energetic? You bet! After spending a few hours with Don, I imagined that an electrified metal pole—like those that rose from the back of bumper cars—must have been positioned somewhere between his shoulders, hooking him into a supercharged grid.

Some might have found Don's energy exhausting. I found it . . . well, energizing.

Don found a receptive ear in me. Within our first hour together he'd told me that he'd been married and divorced, then swiftly remarried and happily wed eight years. Bus driving wasn't his full-time gig; he had "a lot of irons in the fire," he promised me. He was in his forties but looked much younger: his face radiated a good cheer that erased several years. As Don told it, he had suffered the slings and arrows of outrageous fortune but withstood them with sunny resolve.

"I used to let every little thing get to me," he said. "Got a molehill lying around? I'd make a mountain of it."

As for his tutelage, he set his expectations at the correct amperage, *low*, and expressed delight with my elementary driving skills. A clean left turn where I swung the back end to avoid cars parked in the turning lane would earn effusive praise from Don.

"That's it, Craig, keep the nose angled towards the yellow line, good, good, now mind your backswing—these big boys swing a good four feet, so watch out you don't slam into that Nissan parked at the curb—right, right, get the wheel centred . . . *bango!* Now *that's* a textbook left-hand turn."

This was a manoeuvre bus drivers had to complete several times a day, but Don would react as if I'd somehow cobbled together a cold fusion generator out of stray dashboard parts.

"That was one fan-*freaking*-tastic turn, I'm telling you!"

Don was the very best kind of teacher: knowledgeable and

helpful and genuinely kind. He was even supportive during the "pre-trip": an exhaustive inspection that drivers perform before putting their buses on the road each morning.

"This tire looks to be full of air, Don."

"Give it a bang with your broom to check the inflation, okay?"

Obediently, I'd give it a whack.

"That's a real good bang! I like that. Now bend down and take a look at the undercarriage."

"I don't see any ruptured hoses or dripping fluids, Don."

"Outstanding!"

The first few afternoons I trained in a busette, also known as a HandiBus—or mockingly, a short bus. All buses have a seven-mirror system: two on the driver's side, two on the passenger's side, a pair of convex fisheye mirrors telescoping off either side of the hood. Number seven is a long rectangular mirror bolted above the windshield—colloquially known as the "riot mirror."

"Keep your eyes moving between all seven mirrors," Don instructed. "Like you're watching a never-ending Ping-Pong match."

The rest of the week I drove a big bus with a wooden placard on the bumper reading STUDENT DRIVER. This was the bus I figured I'd drive once the school year started—the same kind I'd ridden as a student years ago. The training bus was the standard seventy-two-seater with the engine in front (there were also eighty-eight-seat "hognose" buses, with the engine in back, but I never drove one of those). Its steering wheel was nearly the size of a bicycle tire. I learned all about "back swing": because the final seven-odd feet of a school bus protruded beyond the rear tires, the back of the bus swung out a good four feet during a turn. Bus companies pay millions every year to owners whose vehicles get clipped by bus drivers failing to compensate for this—and of course, the consequences are even worse if a driver cuts a turn too fine and sideswipes innocent pedestrians waiting at a crosswalk.

Don took me to the overflow lot at the Calgary Zoo and set up pylons to navigate around. At first I was nicking them with the bumper and sending them flying, but in time I developed a sense of the bus's size and how to compensate for it. Then there were some white-knuckled training runs through downtown Calgary in the heat of rush hour. Don had to gently commandeer the wheel a few times, but by the end of the week I'd got the hang of it.

Finally, we drove through neighbourhoods to practise pick-ups and drop-offs. These were the most common, but also the trickiest part of everyday driving duties. You had to perform a dozen small tasks sequentially—including hazard lights on, Stop sign activated and flashing, the bus in park and the parking brake engaged—for every pickup. And you had to be watching the students on board your bus, making sure the correct number got off and crossed the road safely. For practice pickups, Don encouraged me to imagine welcoming my students on board. Each pickup became a little skit. If we were in a ritzy area I might throw open the door and say,

"Why hello, young Master Scroggins Fitzhugh the Third! My, but isn't that a fetching cravat you're wearing."

Don would jut his jaw and affect the demeanour of a trust-fund brat.

"Silence, peasant! If you must know, I was bequeathed this cravat by Perry Thriftwhistle following his unfortunate demise in a chateau fire." Don's nostrils dilated. "I say, this bus smells atrocious. Have you been carting about the poors?"

"I did pick up a boy whose father made his fortune on an Internet startup."

"Oh! Most dreadful. *New money.* When I tell Papa he will be ever so angry. I expect he will thrash you within an inch of your life, driver."

If we were on the outskirts practising country pickup procedures, I might open the door and go: "Good morning, Goober Foyle. What's that you've got?"

"Music class today," Don would play along. "This here's ma best blowin' jug."

I discovered that Don sang Christian folk-rock. He gave me his CD, *Be Rich*, and told me about the inspiration behind track number seven: "Winds of Change."

"I spoke to two women who picked up a drifter on a dark road," said Don. "The stranger asked them: 'How long will it be until Jesus Christ sets foot on earth once again?' The women guessed that it would happen in ten years. The stranger replied: 'No. Sooner.' When they looked in the back seat, he was gone."

At the end of each training session I'd peel myself off the vinyl seat like an enormous Band-Aid. On the way home I'd pop Don's CD in and crank the volume.

If you want to be rich, be rich!
If you want to dream then dream the biggest dreams;
If you want to be free, be free!
If you want to love then love with all your might . . .

Listening to Don sing, I wondered: Why *can't* it be that simple? If you want to be rich, you big dope, *BE RICH!* If you're going to bother dreaming at all, then why not dream the biggest dreams?

———

The final afternoon during training, our buzz-cut instructor ran through a slim booklet focused on passengers with special needs. I scribbled down one thing he said: "Everybody is built to different tolerances, okay? You need to accept that in order to drive these routes."

Later, we clustered around a busette in the yard while our instructor tried to teach us how to use a wheelchair ramp. He wrestled a bulky training wheelchair onto the motorized lift and attempted to fasten it down with a series of cumbersome straps.

"Be sensitive to these kids' needs," he counselled. "Help only as much as he or she asks. Don't *over* help."

The demonstration was a disaster. After fussing with the ramp's strap-and-ratchet tie-down system for a few minutes, the instructor flung them aside.

"These are the worst pieces of . . . you guys don't worry, okay? Most buses have the updated restraint system. I'm not really familiar with . . . I've always driven a big bus."

None of us asked questions. We figured we'd drive big buses, the same as our instructor. The trials we anticipated involved boisterous children and a madhouse atmosphere. Small buses weren't our bag.

—

The week following training I took my Class 2 licence exam. Afterwards, I bumped into Don in the bus yard.

"How did it go?"

"Passed it, thanks to you."

He clapped me on the back and flipped his sunglasses down over his prescription lenses. "Dream big, dude!"

4.

The company called me in to discuss the route assignment. The coordinator thumbed through her call sheets and began to fire off possibilities.

"We've got Canyon Meadows. Bonavista . . . Grimhaven . . ."

"Grimhaven's near me."

She pulled up the information. "Route 412. Special needs. Six students. One wheelchair, five walks."

A beat.

"I'll take it."

"You sure?"

Another beat.

"Yeah. *Yeah.* Let's give it a shot."

Like many decisions in my life, this one was seemingly made on a whim. Fate throws down its gauntlet: *Will you accept?* But the truth was, this challenge was fine with me; there were few people more in need of a drastic change.

She handed the printout over. "We can assign you another route if . . . anyway, there's a lot of shuffling at the beginning of the year. Ideally, we match the right driver with the right route, the right kids. The best fit."

I headed over to the yard to pick up my bus. Unit 3077. A yellow busette. It was outfitted with the Q'Straint self-tensioning wheelchair system, a huge improvement over the ratchet-tightened straps that had so vexed our instructor.

"It's one of our nicer cheese wagons," said the mechanic as he handed me the keys.

I sat behind the wheel and read through my assignment sheet. Mine was a split route. Two schools. Four high school students. Two kids in middle school. I read over their conditions. Cerebral palsy. Autism. Fragile X syndrome.

I had little familiarity with these terms, other than what I could recall from movies. The artist played by Daniel Day Lewis in *My Left Foot*—he had cerebral palsy, didn't he? Dustin Hoffman played an autistic character in *Rain Man*. Benny, from that '80s legal drama *L.A. Law* was . . . what, challenged? Was that the right word? I'd never even heard of Fragile X. I scanned each student's program of study. One read: Regular Grade 11. *Regular?* In what context? Others read PLP: Present Level of Performance. Two students were designated ALP, for Adapted Learning Program. Appended to one student's profile was a note: *No sense of direction; cannot be left alone, will get lost.*

My ignorance shamed me. But then, unless you had a

child or a sibling or a parent who was disabled, or unless you
worked with disabled (*differently* abled? Damn, I didn't even
know the right PC-ism) individuals, how high would your
awareness be?

At home I googled "disabled." The definition: *a physical or
mental impairment that substantially limits one or more major
life activities.* This failed to clear things up. A cousin of mine
had fallen down a flight of stairs in her early twenties and
absorbed serious neurological damage; portions of her face
are paralyzed, her speech is slurred and she suffers from
memory loss. Surely she is considered partially disabled, yes?
But hers is a different manner of disability than, say, someone with cerebral palsy, a condition often present at birth.
And even with CP, some people have mild variants that rarely
interfere with their day-to-day—if they, too, are considered
disabled, then surely their disability is of a different order
than that of Christy Brown, the artist in *My Left Foot* who
only had the use of that one foot, or Stephen Hawking, who
is almost entirely paralyzed by Lou Gehrig's disease? There
were so many tiers and gradients to the term. And I'd never
properly considered any of them.

Over the next few days my mind ticked over my own past.
When I was four or five there had been a boy down the block
with a wide-set softness to his features. Everyone said the boy
was "slow." At first I had thought this meant that he couldn't
run fast. But I hadn't been able to run fast either. Did that
mean I was "slow," too? Over time I became aware of the

differences between people, physical and mental. I saw that some people required wheelchairs or seeing-eye dogs; other people might shake uncontrollably or lack the use of one side of their bodies or perhaps reach adulthood unable to complete the same mental tasks most of us will have mastered during childhood.

In my high school, there was a classroom set aside for students with severe disabilities. Most of them had impairments that affected balance, speech and cognitive functioning. A few students wore bicycle helmets. I could never properly gauge their ages. Some of them seemed quite young, their faces unlined and their bodies small, while others appeared to have already reached adulthood. One student wore thick padded gloves: either he hit himself, or the gloves held therapeutic value. Another student with a full moustache kicked a large red ball down the halls while an aide gripped his elbow for balance. The only words he spoke (phonetically transcribed) were: "ar do doo." He repeated these syllables constantly, in an affectless monotone.

"He's saying, 'How do you do?'" his aide told me once as we passed in the hallway.

"Oh, I'm fine," I said cautiously. "How do you do?"

Those three syllables—*ar do doo*—would ring out in the halls from time to time, voiced in mockery of that moustached boy; whenever someone said something stupid or deserving of scorn, a certain element of the student body could be counted on to parrot that phrase. *Shut up, dumbass. Ar do doo! Ar do*

doo! "Retard" was popular, too: an all-purpose word for someone acting goofily. "Stop being a retard," you'd say casually,
laughing at something your friend had done. The mildest of
epithets, indicative of mild annoyance. I was no better. That
word had spilled from my lips plenty of times.

What I realized now, looking back, is that many of us
became *really* uncomfortable around individuals with disabilities. Including me. Such encounters had felt like a door
opening onto a vast realm where I had no foothold, no understanding. It had been best to simply avoid stepping through.
This is what made me hesitate for a beat before agreeing to
the special needs route. It is also what made me say yes.

———

A week before school started, I took the bus out on a dry run.
I navigated around middle-income homes in cookie-cutter
suburban developments, following the map the coordinator
had given. I flagged the ideal pickup spots. Then I went home
to call the parents and introduce myself before the first day of
school. I dialed the first number. My student, a high school
pupil named Antoine, picked up the phone.

"Is this Antoine?"

"Yes"—politely—"that's me."

"Great. Are your folks around?"

"No."

"Okay. My name's Craig. I'm going to be your bus driver
this year."

Dead silence.

"I'm calling to let you and your parents know I'll be picking you up at—"

"School bus?" Antoine said sharply. "The *yellow bus?*"

"That's right."

"The *little* yellow bus?"

I hesitated. Something in the boy's voice . . .

"Yeah, I drive a small unit."

"I ride the *city bus!*" Antoine shouted. "Mom bought bus passes, she said she said she *said!*"

"Okay, fine, that's cool. I'll just speak with your mom and—"

"I don't ride the little yellow bus! I take the city, the citythe citythecitythecity . . . oooooooouuuwwww, I'm so confused."

Normally I would have chalked up his response to teenage melodramatics but Antoine really did sound wretchedly bewildered.

"Antoine, that's your choice."

I felt like an idiot as soon as I spoke the words. There was a good likelihood it wasn't the boy's choice at all.

"I know it's my choice!" he said, and smashed the phone onto its cradle.

That marked my first and last contact with Antoine. He must have got his wish, because he never set foot on the bus all year.

Thankfully, the rest of the calls went more smoothly. The kids' folks were amenable to my pickup locations—most of the spots were right in front of the houses, because rarely do children with special needs congregate at group stops. The last call was to the family of a student named Jake. I reached Calvin, his father, who spoke in a smoke-roughed British accent.

"You've probably read about our family in the paper," he said.

"Not that I know of."

"Then I'd better tell you."

Calvin spoke for five minutes without a pause. As the seconds snipped off the clock and Calvin's story continued to spool out, I thought: *Can I drive this man's son? Am I emotionally equipped for it—no, it's too much, this is just too much . . .*

"So," Calvin said at last, "we'll see you next Tuesday?"

"Yes," I said hollowly. "Bright and early."

FALL

From
"THE SEEKERS,"
an unpublished novel

Nadia Ripley hit the girl hard. Right in the face. Dead . . .
solid . . . *perfect.*

That was the only way to handle your business in places
like the Grand Isle Training School for Girls. If you figured it
was time to punch another ward, you could bet the other girl
was thinking the same thing—so why not get in the first lick?

The other girl's name was Carlene. What kind of name
was that? Sounded like a brand of car wax. Ripley felt a little
bad. Carlene was about the ugliest girl she'd ever seen. Big,
middle-linebacker big, shoulders wide as doorframes. Ripley
wasn't naturally mean-spirited. Life's a vale of tears so why
go screwing with other people's happiness? But Ripley had
caught Carlene eyeballing her when the van dropped her off
a few days ago—Ripley small and skinny and brown-skinned,
her black hair gone greasy from the meds—and knew the big

girl had pegged her as easy meat. Ripley would have to dis-
abuse Carlene of that belief.

But Ripley didn't blame Carlene. Places like this were
designed to drive you nuts. Rats in a cage. Ripley knew this
from experience. Right now it was Grand Isle but last year it
had been the Brookside Institute for Wayward Teens, and
it had been someplace else before that. At each stop Ripley
had run across Carlenes—and much worse. The Carlenes of
this world were big but dumb. Ripley had run across much
more cunning monsters. Often they were the ones running
the place.

Ripley hit Carlene during lunch in the cafeteria, with a
metal serving tray. Carlene was sitting at a table with three
mousy, scabby-elbowed toadies—girls who would have probably made life hell for Carlene in a regular middle school,
calling her Not-so-Lean Carlene. But in here the rules were
different. Being cute and bubbly wasn't worth spit.

Ripley gripped the tray sideways—a solid 1930s-style
chain-gang tray, the tin beaten and nicked—and swung
it into Carlene's face. She thought about taking a little off
it and maybe not wrecking Carlene entirely, but that was
outside-the-walls thinking; in here you got one shot, so you
better make it count. As she swung, Ripley's heel skidded on
a slice of oily processed cheese from her sandwich, which
had fallen to the floor when she squared up the tray. That
slip took some oomph out of the blow but the tray still hit
Carlene's face dead centre, making a dull crunk as the metal

splintered the cartilage of her nose.

Carlene toppled backwards, the light snuffed out of her eyes. Ripley followed her down, fist cocked in case the lights flickered on again. But Carlene was good and out. Two trustees hustled over from the chow line to pin Ripley's arms behind her back and march her off.

As the trustees led her across the quadrangle, Ripley again noted that there were no high cement walls but rather towering nets, the kind you see at driving ranges to stop shanked balls from rolling onto the road. The trustees took her into a building and down a narrow flight of stairs to a row of cells. Each was nine feet long, seven feet wide, six feet high. The floors and wall were concrete. No window. A single bulb burnt inside a metal cage on the ceiling. The door was solid steel with a sliding hatch at the bottom. The trustees didn't say anything. They just put her in a cell and left.

How long would she have to stay here? Ripley could do a few days standing on her head practically, but for the assault she expected a week. That would be rough, but when she got out things would be better and she could mind her P's and Q's until she was eighteen. Three years was a long time to keep your head down and your lips zipped, but she'd manage it. Then they would have to burn her file and let her go.

After a few minutes, the light went off. Ripley sat cross-legged, waiting for it to be switched on again. There wasn't so much as a ribbon of light coming under the door.

Footfalls down the hallway. They stopped outside the door.

"We get blackouts," a voice said. "The power grid is quirky. Sometimes the lights go off for three, four days. Even a week. You should have thought about that."

——

"How are you feeling, Ms. Ripley?"

Ripley blinked. Her eyes were still adjusting to the light. They had taken her out of the punishment cell only minutes ago. She couldn't tell who had released her—her eyes had become so accustomed to the dark that the light, when it finally flooded in from the hall, stung like fire ants.

Time had gone fuzzy in the dark with no way to mark it. Minutes, hours, days all blended together. She had built a box in the centre of her mind and put everything important in it. The box was made of unbreakable material so the rats in her brain—the rats released by the darkness— couldn't get inside. If they did, she'd go crazy. Those rats would squeal and gnaw and spread their infection all through her head. If that happened, she wouldn't care how long they kept her in that cell. They could throw away the key and she'd laugh. But it would be a crazy laugh, a *cackle*. So she built the box strong. She would wait them out. Every one of these bastards. And she would win.

"Ms. Ripley?" That voice again. "Are you okay?"

"Fine, thank you," she said in her best Susie-cheerleader voice.

She faced the man who had summoned her here, to the one-room shack at the edge of the facility. Two chairs. A table. Ripley hadn't seen him before. He wasn't wearing a trustee uniform. He didn't look like he had anything to do with the Grand Isle Training School for Girls.

"You were in that cell for just over three weeks, Ms. Ripley." He folded his hands on the table. "That isn't legal. We can't keep kids in cells. We can't even do it to adults, not for that long. It is cruel and unusual punishment. It's amazing how well you coped."

Why was he telling her this? He spread his hands, as if offering her an apology.

Her eyes were hard. "I'm fine."

"Yes, it would appear you are."

Ripley studied the man closely. He was old, but not *old*-old. Maybe fifty? People wore their age differently. This guy looked tough, weather-beaten. A soldier?

"I know quite a lot about you, Ms. Ripley," he said. "I've read your file."

Ah, yes. Her file. The one that a string of child service workers and foster care parents had been adding to ever since Ripley had become a ward of the state at eight years old. That thing must be as thick as a phonebook by now.

"Was it a good read?"

"It is the record of a resourceful person who has had a lot of bad luck in her young life," he said.

"Too bad you weren't around to tell the judge that. You could have told her I was being resourceful when I hotwired that car. And that being caught was just more bad luck."

The man smiled. A small smile, but genuine.

"Let me ask you something," he said. "If we were to let you out of here—I mean today, right now—where would you go?"

Ripley eyed him coldly. Was he messing with her?

"We might have to," the man went on. "We've broken the law. We should never have kept you in that cell. You could tell someone. We would get in quite a lot of trouble. So just tell me. Where would you go?"

They sat in silence. Slowly, the truth dawned. She didn't have anywhere to go. No home. No family. No real friends.

The man leaned forward. Ripley saw two perfect coins of light dancing in the centre of his eyes.

"Ms. Ripley," he said, "would you like to come with me?"

5.

First day on the job.

The main bus yard was miles away from my house, but the company was okay with drivers parking wherever we liked so long as the bus was safe. I had staked out a parking spot down my block near a condemned home. Not the best idea, in retrospect.

That first day was radiant, sunlight washing the alley running behind the boarded-up house; the alley opened into a field shared by two elementary schools, one Catholic and one public. I saw older kids clustered in groups while the younger kids clung desperately to their parent's pantlegs.

I jacked up the bus hood. Checked the dipstick, hoses, wires, fluid levels, the battery connection. The bus fired up with an earthy rumble. Interior check. Exterior check. All go. Emergency exit operational. Rock and roll.

I steered the busette onto the street. Schoolkids were knotted down the road waiting for their buses. As I slowed down through a school zone, I noticed a teenage boy take a pronounced step away from the curb as the bus got closer.

Whoa, dude, his body language said. *I do not ride that bus, no way no how.*

My first stop was for a high-schooler named Vincent. Grade 12. He was a big kid; he would have made a decent football linebacker, if he'd had the aptitude. Vincent's jeans were perpetually worn beltless; all year long he'd hitch them up. Often they sagged dangerously low, leading one of his bus-mates to chant: *I see London, I see France!* This never fazed Vincent, who, while no exhibitionist, wasn't terribly embarrassed about showing a little skin. His face was perfectly round, his hair neatly trimmed and brushed forward. Every day I would stop in front of his house and wait a minute, sometimes longer, for the front door to open and him to come rumbling down the drive. That first morning he sat directly behind me and said, "I call dibs on thiiiis seeeeeat." It was his regular seat the rest of the year; he sat alone, his body taking up most of it.

"Vincent, right?"

"Yep, thaaaaat's me."

He gripped the padded rail behind the driver's seat and pulled himself forward. He smelled faintly of red licorice. His monotone voice reminded me of Steven Wright, the comedian who told deadpan jokes like, "How much deeper would the ocean be if sponges didn't live there?"

"Ask me aaaaaanything about Star Waaaars," Vincent said, stretching his vowels like taffy. "I know it aaaaall."

In time I'd discover that Vincent really *did* know it all: he had an encyclopedic recall of pop culture, from *Star Wars* to *Family Guy* to *The Simpsons* to *Star Trek* to shows I was too old to know much about, such as *Pokémon* and *Gundam Wing*. If you ever needed to know what Homer Simpson said at the fifteen-minute mark of the tenth episode of the seventh season of *The Simpsons*, Vincent was your man.

I swung back down the street, hung a left and then a right and pulled up in front of a large house. Oliver was waiting. Thirteen years old, with Fragile X Syndrome. I'd already read up on it: an anomaly in the X chromosome; specifically, a failure to express the FMR-1 protein. This can lead to delayed development—physical, intellectual, emotional, or any combination of the three. Oliver's own signifiers certainly seemed to draw a little from columns A, B, and C. Kids with FXS are prone to hyperactivity and anxiety, and can be hypersensitive to tactile stimuli, often withdrawing from even the lightest touch. I would soon notice that Oliver constantly pulled his shirts away from his chest, tweezing and tenting the fabric ritualistically. Individuals with FXS can hit a state of hyperarousal—the fight or flight instinct kicking in—in a heartbeat, often for reasons that aren't noticeably apparent.

As Oliver stepped onto the bus, I felt a palpable crackle of electricity. This boy was *alive* in a quick-twitch, hair-trigger way. I figured a thirteen-year-old with FXS could be a handful, sure, but thirteen-year-olds usually were.

Oliver carried many of the physical traits of FXS. He was short, with protuberant ears and a vaguely elongated face. He had long, thin fingers. Up close, the skin at the edges of his eyes and the corners of his mouth seemed prematurely seamed: in some physical ways he appeared quite a bit older than his age. Other features were simply hereditary, having nothing to do with Fragile X. His eyes were a dark liquid brown. His brilliant blond hair was combed forward in iridescent layers.

Oliver was one snappy dresser. A real clothes horse. American Eagle jeans, Puma sneakers, and a hoodie made up his typical outfit. He kept the hood up most mornings, which gave him the look of a determined little druid . . . that, or a Benedictine monk disillusioned with the Orthodoxy.

"Good morning, Oliver. Nice to meet you."

"Hey."

Vincent and Oliver had ridden the same bus last year. They exchanged gleeful greetings.

"Heeeeeey," Vincent said to Oliver, "are you aware that the Desert Eeeagle is one of the most powerful handguns ever made?"

"Coooool," said Oliver, drawing the word out in admiration and not in mimicry of Vincent's speech. "What are you doing tonight? Sitting at home by yourself?"

"Yeeeah, probably."

"*Cool.*"

After a beat, I realized Oliver wasn't being the slightest bit sarcastic.

The third rider, Nadja, lived in a condo complex on the southern edge of the city. An East Indian girl with eyes and skin the colour of camphorwood, she wore pink on the first day of school. I would soon discover that Nadja wore pink *every* day. Pink coat, pink shorts, a pink barrette in her straight dark hair. Other than a slight speech impediment—which I noticed straight away, but quickly learned was being addressed through speech therapy—and a certain repetitiveness in regard to her word choices, Nadja looked and sounded like any other seventeen-year-old.

She smiled at me. "How are you? I'm very nice. It's a nice day, isn't it?"

Before long I would discover that almost everything in Nadja's world was "nice." Dogs were nice, princesses were nice, days—even rainy ones—were nice, people were nice (unless they weren't), kittens were nice, the drive to school was nice. Everything was nicey-nice, which was . . . uh, nice. It was fun to talk with someone who saw the sun behind every dark cloud and whose emotive palette was dabbed with vibrant oranges and sunny yellows and lip-smacking reds. Which isn't to say that Nadja wasn't capable of registering darker shades, too—she would paint with grim blacks and browns from time to time—but her default setting was happy, easygoing, *nice.*

We drove past big box stores and fast food restaurants. This same exact route, these same potholes and train crossings, would be mine for the rest of the school year. Vincent and Oliver were playing a rousing game of "guns." Their unflinching goal was to vaporize as much of the city as possible, innocent bystanders be damned. Nadja gave them a look as if to say, *Boys. So weird.*

"Hand me another uuuuuzi clip," Vincent said to Oliver.

"How's this?" Oliver reached across the aisle with an imaginary clip.

"Oooooooh yeah. See that Canadian Tiiiire? Acka-acka-acka. Gone."

"Can you make me a scope for my rifle?" Oliver asked.

"With infinite range?"

"Can you *do* that?"

"Of course," Vincent said. "I'm a technomancer."

Oliver sat stunned, waiting for the older boy to elaborate.

"It means I'm a wiiiizard of technology. Hey, did you know that the Gaaaatling Gun was named after a doctor?"

"*Cool.*"

The thought crossed my mind: was it morally correct to stand by as two boys blasted the city to smithereens, even in an imaginary context? But hey, I was their bus driver. My job was to get them from point A to B in one piece; so long as they weren't being cruel to each other, the rest could slide.

Gavin was my final pickup that first morning. He was the same age as Oliver; they both attended the same middle school. The route sheet said Gavin was autistic. Where he sat on the spectrum I could not tell. His mother stood at the front step and waved as her son made his way to the bus. He wore camouflage pants, black Velcro shoes, and sported a majestic mushroom cap of sandy-blond hair.

"Morning, Gavin."

Not once during the entire year did Gavin respond to my unfailing "Morning, Gavin." He wasn't being rude. It was that Gav, as we all came to call him, was basically non-verbal. He managed to express himself in other ways, however; he boasted an expressive lexicon of trilling birdlike noises, whistles, and the occasional *whoa*. He also boasted a collection of "poses," you might call them. He shaped his body into positions such as "The Scarecrow"—holding his arms out, crucifixion-style—or "The Double Crab," where he flexed his biceps like Jack LaLanne.

Most days he seemed pleased to gaze out the window, absorbed in his own thoughts—but if the radio was playing, as sometimes it was, Gav was known to drop a kick-ass air-drum solo. I was always struck by how *clean* Gavin smelled. He'd hop on board smelling of soap and fabric softener and, through some kind of sorcery, would board the bus that same afternoon smelling the same. Most kids, especially the younger ones, tended to smell of dirt and sweat and the residue of whatever bacterial microsites they had diligently investigated that day. Not Gavin. The boy rarely met my eyes head-on (he rarely looked anyone full on), but I'd often catch him looking at me in the riot mirror; if so, he would smile a little wider—he was always smiling—and duck his head sheepishly behind the seat. Most days he seemed to occupy his own happy hospitable world, which evidently shared a permeable barrier with my own. It was a lovely moment when the sun split through those particular clouds, allowing Gavin and me to truly see one another.

I drove down Gavin's block and onto the main drag. The CB crackled: drivers radioed dispatch about late pickups and no shows, traffic jams, the odd Code Yellow. Apprehensive about their first day at school, the kids rode in silence. I dropped Vincent and Nadja at the high school. Afterwards I took Oliver and Gavin to their middle school. Their teachers were waiting outside when the bus arrived.

"Have a good day, huh? See you guys after school."

Driving home, I found myself assessing my performance as one might following a first date. Had I come off too strong? Too . . . what, *needy*? Nosy? For some absurd reason I was worried that the kids would find me dull and give me a Roman Coliseum-style thumbs down. *Our driver is a crashing bore. Have him fed to the lions at once!*

I shook my head disbelievingly. Had I really spent the morning trying to impress *kids*? Truly, mine was a rich and satisfying existence.

——

The fifth student on the bus was Jake.

He was sixteen the year I drove him. That would make him what, twenty-two today, as I write this? Hard to imagine. An adult. Old enough to vote, smoke, drink—though I'm pretty sure he doesn't drink, not now, likely not ever.

Jake has cerebral palsy. The medical designation for his classification of CP is called spastic quadriplegia, the result of an upper motor neuron lesion that prevented the spinal cord receptors from receiving a key amino acid. Symptoms included hypertonia (involuntary spasms), muscular rigidity and abnormal muscle tone. "Quadriplegia" means all four of his limbs are affected. It's progressive, which is to say that it gets worse over time. The year prior to us meeting, Jake had started to use an electric wheelchair. Until then he had been mobile enough to get around on his own.

Calvin, Jake's father, was the last parent I had spoken to during those introductory phone calls. He said his family had recently been in the local paper. Then he told me why.

"Four months ago, my son Jake and my wife were struck by a drunk driver not far from where we live," Calvin said. "They were out for a walk. My wife was killed. Jake's injuries were extensive. One of his lungs collapsed. The other had a hole in it. There were lacerations to the liver, bruising to the heart and kidneys. He suffered damage to his pancreas and lost two-thirds of his spleen. Two pelvic fractures. Broken nose. Cuts and bruises all over. If it were you or me? We'd be dead."

Over the following weeks I'd pieced together the family's recent history. They had moved to Calgary from Cornwall, England, drawn by the prospect of improved health care for their son. They had bought a house in the burbs. Calvin, a carpenter, found employment with a kitchen remodelling company. His wife maintained household affairs and kept a running dialogue with Jake's doctors about his treatments.

Other information I was able to cobble together from local news reports and Internet searches. At 8:20 pm on a weeknight in 2008, Jake, his mother, his younger sister Molly and a family friend were out for a walk, something they did many nights. A black 2006 Dodge Durango tore down the street, skipped the curb and collided with them. Jake was struck glancingly and thrown from his chair. The family friend absorbed serious injuries. Molly was largely unhurt. Jake's mother was hurt very badly. The truck veered back onto the road and accelerated away. Jake's wheelchair remained embedded in its grille.

The driver—a man who lived in the same suburb, and who had been drinking in a bar not far from his home—parked his damaged vehicle in the alley behind his house. He covered the truck with a blue plastic tarp, the kind used to keep firewood dry—a half-assed job, since he was three sheets to the wind. Witnesses helped police locate the residence. The man refused to submit to a Breathalyzer test. Evidently he'd wet himself—but whether that had happened before, during or after the collision remained unclear. His licence had been suspended because of a prior DUI. He eventually had eleven charges brought against him, including Impaired Driving Causing Death and Failure to Stop at the Scene of an Accident (knowing that a person had been injured).

Jake was transported to the hospital with serious, non-life-threatening injuries. He was put into a medical coma and remained in that state for two weeks. By the time he woke up, his mother had passed away.

I first met Jake on the second day of the school year; his father had driven him on the first. The accident that took the life of Jake's mother had occurred four months ago. I pulled up beside the house in a new subdivision, the sort where every tree was a sapling and some of the lawns had been laid down so recently that the sod hadn't knit together yet. The pickup truck in the driveway had a bumper sticker that read: MY KID CAN KICK YOUR KID'S ASS.

I angled the bus's front tires into the curb, as was mandatory on any downhill park. Flicked on the hazards, set the parking brake. Then I swung the doors open—I loved cranking the mechanism to swing those double doors wide, the ultimate *bus-driver* move—hopped out and dropped wooden blocks under the back wheels as a final precaution.

The garage door rattled up. Calvin—athletic, handsome, with the sharkish face of a career criminal from a Guy Ritchie film—came down the wooden ramp connecting the garage's elevated inner door to the floor. He waved and said:

"He'll be out in a minute."

I lowered the wheelchair ramp. Jake was still getting ready

inside the house. His father held the door open, making an *Arriba, arriba! Ándale!* gesture. A young girl—Jake's sister, surely—was hurriedly brushing his hair.

Soon Jake was rolling down the ramp. He piloted (that's the only word to describe Jake's driving style: he worked that joystick like a fighter pilot banking his jet into a tactical turn, desperately fighting the wind shear) a sleek electric wheel-chair with heavy-duty springs. Satchels carrying books and binders hung off the back. He accelerated at breakneck speed and took a corner poorly, one tire clipping the wall.

Jake was a teenager with dark hair, expressive eyebrows, brown eyes, and a face that seemed too threadbare for our country's winters. At sixteen, he was slender—as he will likely be his whole life, not because he watches his weight, but because for him eating can be a chore. His face hinted at future handsomeness: it was there in the prominent cheekbones and aquiline nose. But his eyebrows were too wild and his hair still possessed that baffling teenage tendency to stick up in unruly cowlicks; no matter how many times Jake's father or caregiver ran a comb through it, Jake usually rolled out of his house with at least one sprig jutting at a quizzical angle, like the mast of a sunken ship slanting above the waterline. He wore a tee-shirt, loosely tied sneakers and tear-away athletic pants. A neoprene-padded splint was fastened around his right arm.

I cannot say what I expected. A teenager so worn down by an accumulation of losses that he was glasslike? Broken-hearted and defeated and shell-shocked? Writing this now,

I can say that, yeah, some days Jake *was* glasslike. Other days he raged. And into any conversation, no matter how innocuous, there would seep traces of a soul-deep broken-heartedness. But in the hundreds of hours we eventually spent together that year, on the bus and off, Jake never once seemed defeated. No, not *once*.

"This is your new bus driver. His name is Craig," said Calvin by way of introduction.

"Good morning, Jake."

Jake smiled. "Well, good morning, Craig."

Have you ever met someone and immediately thought: *the two of us, we're gonna get along like bandits?* That's how it happened when I met Jake. I felt an instant, almost audible *click*.

"He'd like to be at the front of the bus," Calvin told me. "His last driver went over railroad crossings and rattled him all to hell."

I'd already installed the wheelchair straps to the right of my own seat. Once Jake's chair was secure, Calvin crouched beside his son. He slipped his hand round the back of Jake's neck and pressed their foreheads together.

"Stay positive, Jake. Positive, positive, positive."

After Calvin left, I pulled onto the street. Dispatch radioed for my whereabouts.

"Running a few minutes behind," I radioed back.

"Sorry," Jake said in his lilting British accent. I came to love the Briticisms he'd work into our conversations: his cellphone wasn't hung on a strap, for example, but rather a "lanyard." When his wheelchair broke, he didn't need to get it fixed, but rather "seen to." He also used the word "lovely"—a word that my grandfather, an expat Brit himself, had been fond of.

"What are you sorry for?" I said. "I ought to know how to strap your chair in. It's my fault we're running late."

He smiled gratefully. I noted the bump on Jake's nose where the broken bone had healed but otherwise, I thought, he looked good. A lot better than I would have.

We retraced our route from the day before. I had thought that would be the most terrible part of the job: the same route, every day. I used to watch bus drivers or subway conductors and think: *Lord, what misery!* Tracing one paved loop every damn day, or shunting a big metal worm full of commuters through dark tunnels under the city. What I found was that, yes, the monotony of the roads *was* deadening. But what happened on board the bus kept the boredom at bay.

The second day, Vincent brought a *Simpsons* comic book on board. This led to a rousing debate, everyone chiming in on their favourite episodes.

"The *Cape Fear* one," Jake said eagerly. "The one where Sideshow Bob keeps stepping on rakes."

"Oh I liiiiike that one," said Vincent.

"Did you guys ever see the one where, uuuhhh, where uhhh . . ." Oliver's face morphed into a frown. "The one time where, uuhhh, when, when, that one show where Peter Griffin gets into a fight with a chicken?"

"That's *Faaaamily Guy,*" Vincent corrected him.

Oliver laughed. "Oh yeah. Ha! That was great!"

The Simpsons and *Family Guy* were beloved by everyone except for Nadja, who much preferred *Hannah Montana* and (archaically) *West Side Story.* Oliver was a video game nut. Jake was an obsessive fan of *Homestar Runner* and a British show called *Red Dwarf.* Vincent was hooked on *The Transformers,* Japanese anime, Monty Python and anything to do with World War I or II—plus the conceivable outcomes of world wars III, IV, V and beyond, which Vincent assured us would be fought by technomancers, cyborgs and flesh-eating robots who would enslave however many hapless humans were still shambling around.

The realization dawned on me. I was driving a bus full of . . . *nerds.*

I could say this with utter conviction because I am one of the biggest nerds you'll ever meet. We nerds can smell our own. I could chime in about every pop culture touchstone those kids brought up. And not just old-timey stuff: *Oh, so you kiddos like wrestling, do ya? In my day I'd watch Whipper Billy Watson tussle with Haystacks Calhoun; I'd buy a bag of horehound candy for a hay penny from the concessionaire,* etcetera and so forth. The truth was, I *still* watched wrestling. If I'd been your stereo-typical bus driver, the kids may as well have been speaking Sanskrit. But their conversations lay squarely in my wheel-house. Hallelujah! Rarely has a case of arrested development as profound as mine paid such handsome social dividends.

That second morning, I pulled into the high school and let Vincent and Nadja off. Then I unstrapped Jake's chair and let him guide it onto the lift. As I lowered it for him, my gaze drifted over to the football field. A quartet of goths were tossing a Frisbee around. There was something hilarious about guys with flowing hair and black trenchcoats engaged in athletics. They resembled pasty long-shanked bats with their unbuttoned coats flapping around their ankles.

"Oh, man. That right there," I said, angling my chin towards them, "is a YouTube sensation waiting to happen."

That was the first time I got a laugh out of Jake. He had the most wonderful, infectious laugh—it bubbled up from the soles of his feet, a total body event. From that moment on, Jake's laugh became the equivalent of auditory cocaine: I'd do just about anything for a fix. Jake, bless him, was the most generous dealer an addict could ask for. Sometimes when I really got on a roll, Jake would be clutching his sides, heaving, begging me: "Please, stop it. I can't . . . I can't *breathe*."

"Are they friends of yours?" I asked, nodding towards the goths.

"Everyone's my friend."

He didn't say this with pride; he was stating an obvious fact. Of *course* everyone was his friend. Duh. He was the kid in the wheelchair whose mother had died. Who except the most towering prick *wouldn't* be his friend?

6.

I turned out to be a pretty good bus driver. Nobody was more shocked by this development than me. Other rookies didn't fare so well. During those first days and weeks, the CB radio was constantly squawking with Code Reds. The fleet of buses absorbed a junkyard's worth of dents and dings. Reams of accident claims were filed. This was standard for the start of any school year, where at least 25 percent of the drivers were fresh hires.

More than a few drivers begged off their special needs routes, too; this, I discovered, wasn't that uncommon. One morning in mid-September, two weeks into the year, a driver called in a Code Blue—the code for a non-specific serious emergency. Code Blues were broadcast over the radios of the entire special needs fleet: we shared channel one, while the big buses used channel two. It was mandatory to have our radios on at all times. That day, the following conversation

was heard by every driver and every student on board every
bus on the road tuned to channel one.

DRIVER: Code Blue!

The words were so loud that the female driver's voice dis-
solved into static.

DISPATCH: Clear the airwaves. Driver, go ahead with the
Code Blue.
DRIVER: This kid . . . it's the same damn kid every day . . .
he's taking his goddamn pants off.

When the call came through that morning, only Gavin
and Oliver were on board; I had dropped the others off by
then. Both boys listened intently.

DRIVER: This kid . . . this *kid* . . . ripping his goddamn pants
off. I'm going to quit, I swear! I shouldn't be expected to
deal with this every day. Why should we have to put up
with this shit?

The driver's voice held a wounded belligerence, as if she
were being subjected to an unfit work environment. I glanced
in my riot mirror and saw Oliver withdraw into his seat, his
knees tucked into his chest as if the woman's voice was physically hurting him.

DRIVER: This kid whipping off his pants is fucking bullshit!
DISPATCH: Calm down. Watch the language.

The woman continued to broadcast her batshittery across the airwaves, into every bus in our fleet, as if under the impression she was giving a rallying cry: *We don't have to put up with neurologically impaired children taking their pants off, people! It's offensive, and we deserve better!*

As she continued to shriek into the microphone I did what I hoped every other driver was doing: I switched the mic off.

"How's it going?" I asked Oliver.

"I'm not really talkative in the morning," he said, staring out the window.

"Okay, I get it. But you shouldn't worry about anything you heard."

"I'm not." A tight shrug of his shoulders. "I'm cool."

We drove in silence. After a minute Oliver said, "The driver sounded angry."

"She's a dingbat, Oliver. She sounded like a real . . . a diva."

"What's a diva?"

"Well, a diva's a . . . *hmm*. Okay, have you ever heard the expression, *That guy thinks the world revolves around him?*"

"*Maaaay*be," Oliver said cautiously.

"Well, so okay, the earth goes around the sun, right?"

"Right."

"And the sun is the most powerful force in our solar system, right?"

"Right."

"And so, we're kind of all alive here on earth because of the sun. It keeps us warm and helps things grow."

"Right."

"So basically, Oliver, a diva is someone who thinks the world revolves around them, so they think—"

"That they're the sun!" he said.

"Yeah, but . . ." I glanced at the mirror and realized Oliver understood; I could practically see the light bulb switch on in the boy's head. "Yeah. Exactly."

"I'm a diva," Oliver said.

"What?" I laughed. "Wait, *you're* a diva?"

"Totally. Look at my jeans." Oliver stretched one of his legs out; it was sheathed in tight denim. "They're my sister's. I stole them. I look good in skinny jeans."

I feigned surprise. "Stole them? You thief!"

Oliver stretched both legs out, catlike. Gavin peeked over the seat at him; his fingers crept over the seat back as a smile touched the edges of his lips.

"So what's with that belt?"

"It's a karate belt," Oliver said offhandedly. "I wear it with my sister's jeans. I'm a *diiiiiva!*"

I was so amused by Oliver's diva persona that I barely took note of the small blot on the road ahead—and by the time I did, it was too late. Recognizing what it was, I made a slight adjustment of the wheel in hopes of avoiding it. But alas, the tires burred right over it.

"That was a rabbit," Oliver said, wide-eyed.

As a bus driver, I had one major shortcoming: I ran over a lot of roadkill. You must understand: I didn't run over *live animals*. But I did possess an unerring accuracy for running over dead ones. And—in the terrible way that events unfold in nightmares—the more I tried to *stop* doing it, the more chronic this tendency became. I'd try so hard to avoid squishing the expired animals that I'd overcompensate and somehow end up running them over squarely.

The city's roadkill knew no safe haven that year. I was a menace. I'd go on to flatten a dead crow, re-squash a squirrel, and run over the bloated carcass of what might have been an expired possum. On all but one of those occasions the bus was empty, thank heavens. When spring rolled around a hapless sparrow flew directly into the bus's grille and exploded like a snowball chucked at a chain-link fence. I nearly developed a complex. Were the city's suicidal animals hurling themselves at my bus on purpose? Did I *yearn* to squish dead animals— did I consider it a thrill, deep in my most secretive heart?

I envisioned a poster for one of those 1970s exploitation flicks that randy teenagers used to watch at the drive-in: *The Bloody Bus.* There I was, boffo-eyed and surely "hepped up" on "goofballs," rabid foam escaping from the sides of my mouth as I loomed behind the wheel of my busette, which had a skull-and-crossbones motif emblazoned on the hood.

THE WHEELS OF THIS MADMAN'S BUS
CRAVE INNOCENT RODENT BLOOD!

So, yes, on this first occasion it was a rabbit. A fat grey hare in the middle of the road with its broken neck twisted around so that, awfully, it was facing its own bottom. I steered wide, hoping it would pass harmlessly between the tires. But I swung *too* wide, missing the rabbit with the front tires only to pancake it with the rear ones. There was no jolt, no noise to speak of. Only a momentary skid while the tire did its grim work.

The boys' heads swivelled back. Oh, what a sight! The rabbit (forgive me, but there is no pleasant way to frame this)—the rabbit had *unravelled* across the road. A bright red skidmark. Gavin inhaled sharply: the sound a person makes before holding their breath underwater. How could I express to him that I hadn't meant to hit that poor bunny, and that it had already been stone dead?

"Oooooh-kay," I said mock-jovially. "That was a bit of a slip up, wasn't it?"

"That thing's just . . . *gone*," said Oliver. "Wowsers."

We continued to the school in silence. I flicked the CB radio back on; the airwaves were silent, the woman's hateful harangue mercifully over. I hoped she had been fired; maybe we would even receive a memo from dispatch, warning us to be sensitive over the broadcast channel.

I brooded over this as Oliver and Gavin gathered their belongings and made their way off the bus. As he passed,

Gavin reached out and trailed his hand along my shoulder. The faintest touch, so light that I wasn't sure he'd made contact. When I looked up, his gaze was pinned on something outside the bus, his head cocked at a questioning angle. He swept past me carrying that clean dryer-sheet smell, and made a soft, noncommittal sound—a single note, starting high and dipping to a lower octave. The sound lasted no longer than a heartbeat, but I took it as one of commiseration. For what? The rabbit I had run over? The woman on the radio? Impossible to say. Perhaps there was no connection to anything that had happened at all. Gavin had touched me simply because he'd wanted to, in that moment. I watched him walk onto the schoolyard, kids dashing this way and that, engaged in games that Gavin showed no interest in joining. He circled the trashcan in front of the main doors three times, hunching his shoulders to help him navigate it in a tight radius. He stopped and stared again at that indeterminate point in the sky, his gaze pinned to something I could not see.

7.

Signs hang in every bus on the fleet. They are mandatory. If one gets torn or disappears, a new sign is put up quickly in its place. The signs say: IF YOU ARE BEING BULLIED TELL YOUR DRIVER.

There were no bullies on my bus. That's not to say that my seven passengers always got along, buddy-buddy—there was friction and there were disagreements. But any conflict was fleeting, and all disputes were resolved equitably. Nobody was doling out wet willies or purple nurples or playing any of the maliciously cruel mind games most of us either executed or suffered at some point during our childhoods. In truth, I'm not sure the kids on my bus *knew how* to bully. They had little of that amped-up physicality common in most teenagers: the pushing, the purposeful invasion of space, those feigned "made you flinch" punches (followed by two for actual flinching). Sure, Vincent was a big guy and he might bowl someone over, but if so it was accidental and he would always apologize for it. You might think that the bullying gene wasn't in their DNA . . . but that would be an underestimation of them. All I'm saying is, I never saw evidence of it.

Sure, sometimes feelings were hurt, but rarely intentionally. I recall a conversation between Vincent and Jake:

"Jake, it must be aaaaaawful not being able to walk."

Jake—who was intellectually far ahead of anyone else on the bus—took Vincent's question evenly, understanding he meant no harm.

"I used to be able to walk when I was younger."

"Do you knoooow that the technology of medicine is improving sooo much that you could have roboooootic legs in a few years?"

"The problem with my disease isn't in my legs. It's in my brain."

"Oh . . . well, did you know that meeeedical technology may be able to fix damaged brain cells, too?"

"Yay for medical technology," Jake said, then continued in a cheesy TV voiceover voice: "We can rebuild him. We have the technology."

After I'd dropped off the other kids and Jake and I were alone, he opened up. We had known each other a while by then, so it was not uncommon for us to share intimacies. *Bus secrets*, we called them. We entered the Cone of Silence.

"Why would Vincent ever think . . . robotic *legs*?"

There was no use stating the obvious. Vincent was a dreamer who believed that if it could happen on *Star Trek*, well, it could just as easily happen in 2009.

"He was only trying to be helpful."

"Hopeful."

"I said helpful."

"I heard you the first time, but okay." Jake stared at the window; a leaf was trapped in the insulation strip, fluttering against the glass. "Robotic legs. Hm. Do you think so?"

"You never know."

"Sure you do," he said wearily, and I didn't bother arguing.

———

Bullying is at its root about social positioning, and teenagers can be hyenas: the ultimate opportunistic hunters. The kids on my bus occupied the lowest rung on the food chain—so low, in fact, that most predators steered clear altogether. But some of the kids at their schools or in their neighbourhoods hadn't got the memo that reads: *You don't hunt the easy meat.*

The first time I encountered bullying directed towards the kids on my bus was while driving through Oliver's neighbourhood in early October.

"Oh no," Oliver peeped from the back. "I'm in trouble."

He was looking up the road, where a big bus was emptying its cargo at the top of his street.

"Those kids are going to pick on me," he said.

I glanced in the riot mirror at Oliver. He was a tough kid

with a chip on his shoulder. He didn't strike me as the type to back down. In fact, he had a little of the Napoleon complex in him. But the bone-deep worry in his voice caught my attention.

"Sit up, will you?" I said casually. "It's not safe, crouched down in your seat like that."

Oliver refused to do so until we had turned the corner.

"You shouldn't woooooorry what people say," said Vincent. "It makes them look stuuupid, not you."

"It's like my dad says," Jake agreed. "Life's hard, but it's harder if you're stupid."

I dropped Vincent off and swung the bus around to drop off Oliver. His antagonists still lurked at the corner. A look of abject dread bloomed on Oliver's face.

"Drop me off at my house," he pleaded. *"Please."*

I relented. As we passed the boys, I saw them pointing at the bus. *There goes the retard bus*, I heard one of them say. A dark curtain fell over my thoughts. My fingers tightened on the wheel. I couldn't recall ever being quite so enraged as I was at that moment.

"Just a sec."

I pulled over. Put the bus in park. My body felt stiff. Anger had tensed me up and turned me into a kind of marionette, not fully in control of my limbs. I had to remind myself to stay under control: I, too, had done plenty of mean-spirited things as a kid.

"What are you doing?" Oliver said, petrified.

"Back in a jiff," I said robotically.

I walked up to a trio of bony hoodlums-in-training. Baggy-assed jeans, baseball caps pointing off their heads at sideways angles. They were roughly Oliver's age. These were kids from his street, kids he'd presumably grown up with. Perhaps they had been making fun of him for years.

"Something funny, guys?" I said, dimly aware that I was grinding my molars.

"Naw," one of them said.

"You weren't laughing at the bus? Pretty sure when I drove by I saw you all howling."

"We weren't laughing, man," another one said. Sullen, challenging. *Man*. They were glancing up the street, at their homes no doubt. They were close enough to holler if this bus driver did anything weird.

"There's nothing funny about the bus, right? Am I right? It's like any other bus, isn't it? Or do you guys find buses funny?"

"Nuh-uh," they said in unison.

"If so, I could take you down to the bus yard. *Tons* of buses there. You'll laugh until you cry, it'd be so funny."

"I wouldn't go anywhere with you," one of them said.

And suddenly, my anger cooled. I realized it was stupid, trading barbs with these boys. What was that saying? *You can't fight other people's battles.* Sensing I'd made Oliver's life harder and hating myself for it, I turned back to the bus.

Over time I came to see that Oliver got picked on a lot, often because he had the temerity to try to fit in with his schoolmates. At the end of each day the special needs teacher led her students through the chaotic schoolyard to the bus queue. Sometimes Oliver would peel away from his group and drift towards a pocket of other students. He'd sidle up next to a kid and either clasp a chummy hand round his shoulder or patiently wait to be acknowledged. Sometimes the other boy appeared to say something off-handedly polite before dismissing Oliver. Once a boy stepped on Oliver's toes—Oliver played it off by laughing and hooking a thumb at the kid as if to say: *this guy's a real card!* Another time a boy said something that made Oliver deflate like a botched soufflé. He slunk onto the bus, pressed his forehead to the window and wouldn't speak the whole way home.

Despite the fact that my first attempt ended—predictably—in failure, I had quite a few "little chats" with people that year. I'd stop, get out of the bus and confront someone, then hop back on still steaming. Once I doubled back three blocks to confront a fellow I'd spied chortling at the bus in a strip mall parking lot. When I pulled in, he seemed surprised. He had been sitting on a curb eating a submarine sandwich. He stood up as I walked towards him, the two halves of the sandwich yawning open in his hands.

"What were you laughing at a minute ago when I drove by?" I said.

"Nothing," he said. "Can't remember."

It seemed an honest answer. I wouldn't have been surprised to discover the fellow had the memory of a goldfish.

"You're sure you weren't laughing at the bus?" This had become my standard line, and I gave it the Joe-Pesci-in-*Goodfellas* treatment. "You laughing at the bus? You think buses are funny?"

"Nothing's funny," he said shiftily.

"You sure seemed to be yukking it up at something."

At this, the fellow said—I'll never forget it: "I saw a bird."

"You saw a bird, did you? A *funny* bird?"

"It was flying sort of funny."

I'm not sure when it dawned on me that my actions were futile—only that it *did* dawn. There would always be pointers and laughers. When we see this in children, it's understandable. But that year of bus driving taught me that far too many of us reach adulthood still thinking there's something inherently hilarious about disabilities. Or it could be the laughter is a kind of talisman, a means of warding off the swarming fear and confusion that many must have felt as my bus, with its passengers, crossed their sightline.

Before I had this realization, I'd blamed the bus itself—because the bus was a red flag, wasn't it? The short bus. Why couldn't I drive my kids in a big bus? We could blend in, for Heaven's sake! But it was a matter of cost: there weren't enough special needs passengers to make big buses feasible; and the route would have taken several hours to drive if you had to drop thirty or forty high-needs children at their separate schools. Big buses only worked for the other 99 percent. The system was exclusionary but it made sense financially, and as an adult I knew that dollars and cents drive a lot of decisions.

Still, the situation rankled me. The source of my irritation was ungrippable, a pebble in my shoe. If you glanced at Nadja or even Oliver—I mean, there was no strong physical indication that those kids *had* special needs. Sure, if you were aware of the markers of Fragile X, you might have spotted them in Oliver. If you saw Vincent walking down the street and weren't observant enough (as most of us aren't) to spot his choppy, stuttering steps and pigeon-toed gait, you would likely have had no clue that he attended special classes at school. But the bus . . . it was the scarlet letter. A big, fat, unmissable target—and anyone who stepped inside or off it was a target, too.

Seething, I'd wonder: Why not let my kids ride in a big bus? That way they wouldn't have to exist under the microscope, subject to all the glances and giggles as the 'tard bus rolled by. A few years before driving the bus I'd worked as an in-class aide at a school with a high immigrant population. I worked in classes where children who weren't yet fluent in English were having difficulty keeping up. I helped those kids, which helped the teacher. But those kids weren't put in separate classes: they were mainstreamed, the assumption being that once their language skills developed they would no longer need help. Yes, certain special needs children will *always* need help, but why not put an aide on a big bus to help the bus driver should those issues arise? Why not have children with special needs ride alongside children who do not share those needs? Wouldn't that be good for all concerned?

It took a while for me to understand that most of the kids on my bus were perfectly happy to be on it.

"Why would I want to ride thaaaaat one?" Vincent said when I floated the idea of him riding a big bus. "None of my frieeends are on it."

Didn't the looks bother him, though? The pointing, the laughing? I'm not sure they did—or if so, my kids didn't notice, didn't mind, or had learned to accept how they were sometimes viewed. As Vincent said: *It makes them look stupid, not us.* Later I learned that some of these kids' parents had offered them the chance to ride a big bus. They could queue with the other students at a group stop and find a regular seatmate. But the kids didn't want that. Perhaps they would change their minds one day, but for now they were happy to be on the small bus. So the problem was one of perspective— my own. I wished for an inclusivity most of those kids didn't necessarily crave (or perhaps, with a maturity outstripping my own, one they understood wasn't feasible). I fell into the trap of wanting to engineer their existence to match my own expectations—I eventually saw that I had became the hectoring movie father who wanted his son to buck up and go to dental school when what the boy really wants is . . . to *dance*!

And you know what? As I soon gathered, the kids could stick up for themselves.

One afternoon they were piling into the bus at the high school. A couple guys walked past in their football jackets.

One of them stopped and stared at the bus.

"What are yooooou looking at?" Vincent said to him.

Football Jacket affected a gimp-legged gait, relaxed his jaw so that his mouth hung open like a drawbridge and went: "Duuuh-deeeerrrr . . ."

Vincent shot out of his seat—when he wanted to, that boy could move. Reflexively, I jumped up and blocked the door.

"Screeeew yooooou!" Vincent hollered at Football Jacket.

Vincent's full weight, all 250 pounds of it, was pressed against me. But—and this surprised me—it was *just* weight, the sheer bulk of him, as if a fleshy armoire were resting on me. If you've ever held back somebody who wants to fight and knows how, you'll be familiar with the weight of a body primed for a punch-up: there's a thrumming, coiled tension. Vincent's body lacked that entirely. Though he outweighed Football Jacket, Vincent could have been quite badly hurt in any confrontation.

"Uhhh-uhhh-deerrrr . . ." Football Jacket continued as his buddy laughed.

That's when Oliver leaned halfway out of the window and, in a sunny voice, said: "You're a tall drink of piss, aren't you?"

There was a moment of silence as we all processed Oliver's words—then the bus collapsed into riotous laughter. Vincent heaved great barrel-chested hoots against me, laughing so hard—and I was struck by my own paroxysms of glee—that we nearly toppled out of the door.

"Drink of *piiiiss!*" Vincent howled.

"Stop!" Jake was quaking, his cheeks stained with tears. "You muh-must . . . !"

Football Jacket tried his mockery again, but with less confidence and enthusiasm.

"You should probably just go," I told him with a faux-sad shake of my head.

Football Jacket delivered a few more feeble "Deeerrs" as he slunk off. Oliver luxuriated in being the centre of attention, having administered his masterful burn. Nonchalantly, he said:

"Yeah, I thought you guys would like that . . . tall drink of piss. Ha!" A look of understanding spread across his face. "Hey! I get it now. I just got it!"

———

There were a few more confrontations that year. I'm not proud of them. Under normal circumstances I am an even-keeled gent. But circumstances that year were not always normal, and they occasionally overwhelmed me.

The most intense confrontations happened over a two-day stretch in early October. I was parked at the high school after classes. I stood outside the bus lowering the lift for Jake, who was lollygagging. Gavin was gazing out the window at me. I noticed a couple teenagers off my left shoulder, near the doors; they were making faces at Gavin. Their expressions were theatrically outsized—the same faces I often made for

Gavin's amusement, but theirs had a different intent. For the moment, I let it go.

Jake zipped out the doors, crossing behind the mocking boys. "Craig!" he said, and began to fill me in on the events of the day. I helped Jake onto the ramp; the lift motor whirred crankily as it struggled with the weight of Jake's chair. Back inside the bus, I saw one of the boys give Gavin a nasty bug-eyed look. He and his friend sniggered. Gavin's smile persisted. I saw red. Is there anything more upsetting than watching someone being teased when they don't know they're being made fun of?

I gave the little shits a dead-eyed stare through the window. And thankfully, they wandered off.

On edge now, I drove through the parking lot. Adolescent boys in football jerseys were packed into a Jeep with death metal pouring out of its speakers. Elsewhere students were clustered at cars, jockeying for rides home. Such moments always felt strange to me—as if Jake and the other kids were members of a safari tour driving through the African veldt, observing the strange habits of its wildlife.

My eyes scanned a group thirty yards ahead. The guy who caught my attention was handsome, no acne, a pair of aviator sunglasses hooding his eyes. As the bus approached he made that classic "retard" gesture—where you bend your arm at the elbow and let the wrist dangle limply, then thrash your hand against your chest. How had that stupid floppy-handed chest-bash become a universal gesture? Had it been ratified by an International Council of Assholes in Geneva?

I slammed on the brakes. A toxic substance was hurtling through my veins. My skull felt hot, like I was being stung by a horde of fire ants.

Aviator Shades and his two buddies lounged in carefree poses against the bumper of a sports car. Shades was handsome, cloyingly so. High cheekbones and blond hair so abundant that you just *knew* he'd never need a toupée. The sort of cheery, blithe blond jerk who looked as if he'd never known a hard day's toil. I hated him on sight. He seemed to be coated in a fine sheen of bully-mist. There are different kinds of bullies; I can spot the differences, having run the gamut as a younger lad. You've got your dumb bunnies with big swinging fists—the Coke Classic of bullies. You've got your ratlike creeps who ingratiate themselves into a kind of a parasitic arrangement with those aforementioned bunnies, creating an unholy tandem. And you've got bullies like Shades here, who lord their genetic gifts over all and sundry and generally make your life hell whenever you're unlucky enough to fall within their sightlines. They don't even put much effort into it, handling their business with a flippancy that stings all the more for being so casual. They can't be *bothered* with you, but when their attention does turn in your direction, however briefly, they treat you with a careless disregard, as if you belong to some lower order of life.

I got out of the bus and stalked over to Shades, this small god of the parking lot.

"What did you do that for?" I asked.

"Do what?" he said, blasé.

"That move. Whapping your chest. It's funny?" I wheeled on his pals. "What about you guys—you think it's funny?"

We were out in the open air on a fine autumn day, but I felt claustrophobic. Adrenaline was twining swiftly up my spine.

I turned back to Shades and said, "Hey man, you ever see your father get punched in the face?"

Before he could answer, I went on. "Here's the deal. You show up with your father tomorrow, okay? Right here, same time as today. Wait until I drive past. Then the two of you— you and your dad, yeah?—you make that gesture as I go by. If you pair of sunny assholes do that, here's what I'll do. I will get out, walk over, and I will punch your dad right in his fucking face."

I did not say this with a steely-eyed glint or Liam-Neeson-esque sang-froid. There was a lot of sputtering and flecks of spit. But I suppose I made my point. I stalked back to the bus.

"What's the maaaaatter?" Vincent asked as I climbed back on board.

"It's all good. Just needed to say something."

"What?" Jake asked.

"Nothing to worry about, you guys."

Meanwhile, my mind was racing. Had I just threatened a student? I had, hadn't I? Good God. Although it had been more of a hypothetical threat based on an equally hypothetical action on his father's part. Still. What if Aviator Shades' father showed up? Papa Shades. What if Papa was a violent rageaholic who practised Shotokan karate? I'd be combing busted teeth out of my hair for weeks. Plus I'd get canned. Unemployed *and* toothless. What a cheerful prospect. I asked myself: *would* I fight that kid's father if he made that gesture? Surely he'd be mortified to hear what his son had done, but what if he supported his kid and wanted to rumble? Well then, whatever. I'd throw hands with Papa Shades, you bet. Any grown man who made that gesture, I'd do my level best to make sure we both wound up in the hospital.

Naturally, the kids were curious about what had happened. They peppered me with questions. Under normal conditions I'd have been an open book, but in this case I didn't want them to know what had gone down. They might tell their parents, who may harbour the reasonable suspicion that their child's bus driver was slightly unhinged.

Mercifully, the conversation veered away from the event in the parking lot and towards more common topics: TV shows, Nadja's newest drawing, Vincent's latest story. I drove in silence, my mind ticking over the enormity of what I'd just done.

Still edgy the next day, I arrived at the high school early. My bus was empty. Gavin and Oliver had a PD day. The bell wouldn't ring for another half-hour. A gnawing worry compelled me to get there well before the students were dismissed. If a confrontation was going to happen, it was best to make sure that . . . but there was no way, was there? I couldn't imagine the kid's father showing up to take me up on my rash offer. That would be insane—more insane than the offer itself.

I steered the bus into the rear lot where yesterday's encounter had gone down. I scanned the tarmac.

No . . . *way*.

A hundred yards distant stood that familiar, sickeningly handsome face. Beside that face was another one, not handsome at all. A face belonging to a man who could only be the kid's father. Papa Shades, in the flesh.

Where the boy was tall, blond, and good-looking, his father was squat and almost bald. The remains of his hair clung to the base of his skull in determined thatches. I eased on the brakes and stepped out of the bus with my heart hammering. I'd asked for this, hadn't I? Take your lumps, Davidson.

I walked over to Papa Shades and Junior Shades—he wasn't wearing sunglasses today, and his eyes were a washed-out brown; it heartened me to discover that some part of his anatomy wasn't of movie-star quality.

"You the one?" Papa Shades said.

The man had absurdly fat hands. Not hamhocks, not callused or scarred, just bloated. I began to suspect my well-being was not at issue . . . but then, who knew? He might slap the hell out of me with those inflated meathooks and leave me concussed.

"Am I the one what?"

"Gonna beat the shit out of my kid." Papa Shades jutted his chin. "That you?"

I said: "Is that what he told you? Is that how he said it happened?"

"Nevermind what he told me," the father said. "Who do you work for?"

I glanced over my shoulder at the bus. The company logo was emblazoned obviously on its flank.

"What did your son say happened?" I asked.

"Going to punch him in the face, is that it? Put his lights out, yeah? Big tough guy, that what you are?"

"That's what he said? Did he tell you that he did this, too?"

I made The Gesture. The father's face changed. His look was that of a defence counsellor presented with damning evidence previously withheld by his client.

"As I was driving by with my kids," I said. "Yeah, your son did that. What, did you think I would say what I said for no reason? Punch someone in the face for nothing?"

"Yeah, so—" the father said slowly.

"And anyway," I clarified, "I said I was going to punch *you* in the face."

The father stiffened. "Me? That so?"

"That is so. If you came to the school today and you and your son did this"—I made The Gesture again—"as I drove by, I'd punch you. That much is true."

The father was obviously still struggling to process this turn of events.

"Punch another grown man in the face . . . who the hell do you work for?" He put stress on the *who*, as if in chastisement of any company that would hire a lunatic like me.

I faced his son again. "You dragged your dad out here and didn't bother telling him the real story?"

Papa Shades said, "He's not part of this."

I said, "Listen, he's the *main* part of this."

"And you're innocent?"

"Come on," I said to the teenager, who hadn't made a peep.

"Circumstances irrelevant," the father said. "You don't make threats to kids."

"I threatened *you*."

"Even so. I'm talking to the principal. You're fired, man. Finished."

"Fair enough." I didn't feel like apologizing—why the hell would I? *Should* I? "You do that."

I thought that would mark the end of our encounter—but then, something strange happened. Papa Shades took a step towards me. We weren't standing far apart, and that one step effectively halved the distance between us. I couldn't discern his motivations—maybe he'd come to the school expecting a tussle, thinking he'd find a wheezy shambles of a driver he could wipe the floor with. I wasn't anything special, but nor was I a marshmallow. Maybe he was thinking he'd come here to fight and damn it all, he still *wanted* to fight. Or maybe he'd told his kid he would kick my tail and now had to make good on it or stand forever reduced in his boy's eyes. Or who knows, maybe he just wanted to shake my hand. We hadn't had the sort of conversation that should naturally end with a gentlemanly gesture—I'd threatened to punch him; he'd threatened to have me fired—but still. Maybe he was one of those guys who craved the finality of a handshake.

Whatever the reason, he took that step. My first impulse was to stick my hand out in case he actually *did* want to shake—but I hunched my body as I did so, taking a half-assed pugilist's stance. When he saw this, *his* hand came up, too. But not the hand he'd have used to shake; I stuck out my right hand and he raised *his own* right. That hand grabbed my shoulder, his fingers clenching my yellow vest. Which was when it registered: *Wait a second, the guy* does *want to fight!* So I brought my left hand up and locked it around his neck; his skin was burning and rubbery, like a hot water bottle filled with warm lard. There we were, two grown men about to fight in a school parking lot. It was absurd, but evidently it was happening.

"Kick his ass, Dad," Junior said, somehow managing to sound bored. I wondered if he'd wade in and help his pops beat me down. He probably didn't lift a finger when his dad told him to mow the lawn, but he'd happily pitch in on an old-fashioned double-team. It could be a real father-son bonding moment. *Remember the day we beat the tar out of that*

mouthy bus driver, Dad? Oh, you better believe it, sonny boy!
I imagined the school bell ringing and students streaming
from the doors to find me curled up like a potato bug beside
my bus. What an odd mystery I would make.

I waited for the man to take a swing. He didn't. Perhaps
neither of us wanted to. As such, we just staggered around
aimlessly, tugging at each other's clothes. I imagine we looked
like a pair of drunken, quarrelsome winos waltzing around an
oil-drum fire.

After maybe ten seconds of this bewildering dance, we
backed off. We were both sweating and my hair was mussed.
His neck was flushed. He pointed one of his sausage-link fingers at me. *You mind yourself now, you hear?* that trembling
finger seemed to say. *There's more where that came from, pal.*

Had he won? There were no judges to score the bout, but
if there had been, I imagine their scorecards would have read:
LAME. Fine, I figured, let him think he'd won. If nothing else
it would mark an end to the sorry encounter.

"Let's go," Papa Shades said to his son. "He's learned his
lesson."

Bite your tongue, Davidson, I thought. *Let him have this
touching moment with his appalling child.*

Papa Shades tried to throw his arm around his kid's shoulders; Junior Shades shrugged it off. I thought: *May your lives
be filled with wonders beyond measure.*

Walking back to the bus, I couldn't stop shaking. I sat
behind the wheel, gripping it so hard that my knuckles went

white. Why did I keep embroiling myself in my kids' lives in such a stupid, needless way?

Papa Shades and his son got into their car—a pewter-coloured land whale with dust caked on the rocker panels. It pulled out of its parking spot, veering past my bus. Was Papa Shades staring daggers at me? I didn't make eye contact. We were done. *I* was done. It was a zero sum game. Getting into confrontations, threatening people—making myself the ham-fisted protector my kids had never asked for. If I kept at it, I'd wind up with my jaw wired shut before Halloween. A sick, helpless anxiety hived inside my chest. I wondered how the parents of my charges handled the sideways looks, the stage-whispered platitudes masquerading as concern ("Oh, the poor thing . . ."—*thing*, as if their child was ungendered, non-specific, an object of pure pity), the thoughtless, nonchalant cruelties levelled by Aviator Shades and his ilk. A parent couldn't possibly defend their child against all of it; there wasn't enough skin on their knuckles (or mine), enough voice in our lungs, enough strength in our bodies to fight it. We could hurl ourselves against that durable wall of insensitivity, but I'd been trying to do just that and all I had to show for it was a few tense conversations and one sloppy, immature wrestling match.

What was the alternative—*accept* it? I couldn't. But I couldn't keep fighting the way I had been, either. It didn't help me, and, as I finally had to admit, it wasn't helping the kids. If anything, my actions merely called attention to matters they had learned to dismiss, having developed strategies to cope; I was the equivalent of an amplifier, forcing them to hear a frequency they had taught themselves to tune out. And if I got fired—a possibility that was real and chilling—it would deprive me of the few needful hours I spent with those kids every weekday.

Realizing this, I stopped. From that day on, I went cold turkey. Sure, I'd give a side-eye or a glare when I heard disparaging talk, but I forced myself not to escalate matters. *Most* kids get picked on, right? Isn't that the toll of growing up? I told myself this. I had to. You make concessions. You stand down. You're not always capable of changing the world—and sometimes it's hard to protect even your little patch of it, the garden where the most beautiful flowers grow. But you have to trust the resiliency of those flowers. They have made a life in that inhospitable soil, and somehow they manage to thrive.

8.

To my deep relief, Papa Shades didn't call the school and therefore I did not face a reprimand for our pitiful parking-lot scuffle. I spent the following week waiting for the other shoe to drop, the phone to ring, the principal to summon me to his office—thankfully, life continued blessedly apace. I would spot Aviator Shades in the parking lot throughout the remainder of the year, slouching disaffectedly against the hood of his car. I couldn't tell if he was watching me: his sunglasses made it impossible to pinpoint the direction of his gaze. We maintained our distance. I kept my job, and tried to keep my cool.

This resolution was complicated by the fact that, in addition to the kids on my bus being a target, so was the bus itself. And as with bullying of the kids, I struggled to grapple with my outrage over the insult to a vehicle for which, I realized, I had developed an odd attachment.

In the early weeks of October, my trusty steed of the road—good ole 3077—was mercilessly ransacked by neighbourhood hoodlums. I had parked it, as usual, in an alley behind the abandoned home, which was just down the block from my own house. 3077 had gone unmolested since the start of the school year. But one sunny morning as I walked down the alley, I noticed a suspicious sparkle of glass on the ground. The understanding dawned by degrees: busted glass . . . shards of red and yellow plastic? I walked up to my bus. The rear brake-lights had been smashed—the empty sockets peered back at me, black and jagged. The side mirrors had been broken, too: their spiderwebbed surfaces reflected my shocked face.

Some punks had busted holy hell out of poor unit 3077!

The malicious vipers! It was a special needs bus!

The CB radio was still in one piece. I radioed dispatch. There was no way the bus was fit for transport; dispatch told me to bring my crippled vehicle into the bus yard. I sighed inwardly. The repairs would take hours. And that meant I'd have to cool my heels in the driver's common room, surrounded by my fellow cheese-wagon jockeys.

Ugh, that common room. A cramped, fluorescent-lit area next to the mechanics' bays. One long table, cafeteria chairs, a row of vending machines. This space acted as a kind of tractor beam for the very worst bus drivers, those with questionable histories: dental, personal, or otherwise; the drivers who were every kind of *-ist* you could name: sexist, racist, polemicist, you name it. A bigger pack of moaners you would not find. They groused about their route assignments and claimed dispatch was out to get them. They bleated about their bunions and plantar warts. They griped that they ought to start a union to stop "the man" from busting their chops all damn day.

I drove to the yard nursing the slim hope that the common room had been populated by bad eggs on my past visits. It had to be better this time, didn't it? Entering the room, I was dismayed to recognize many of the same faces: how could their buses always be broken? Were they dumping sugar into their own gas tanks? I handed my keys to the clerk behind the counter; she filled out a work order and told me the repairs would take four hours at least.

I sat dejectedly and opened a book. My attention was soon stolen by two middle-aged drivers engaging in some randy sex talk.

GRASPING LECH: So, you wanna take my bus for a test drive?

HUNGRY HAUSFRAU: A ride, uh? A ride would be real niiiiice.

LECH: I've got a big ole bus with the engine in back. It's a pusher. It's a great big ole thing.

HAUSFRAU (*with a high whooping laugh*): I bet you'd just push it right on in, wouldn't you?

LECH: Oh, you bet. You've got to have a little cushion for all that pushin'.

HAUSFRAU: You better knock the cobwebs off it first!

Watching this exchange was like tuning in to a nature documentary revealing the mating rituals of sea slugs; I was simultaneously horrified and transfixed, unable to look away. Oh hell, why couldn't I be happy for these human catastrophes? Why couldn't I support their brazen horndoggery, however disturbing? I probably wouldn't want to watch sea slugs get busy, either, but I wouldn't stake the moral high ground against it. So what if two perspiring middle-aged bus drivers wanted to talk dirty to each other, if only to avoid gazing into the murky abyss of their own souls? Go with God, you two! Have at it. Couldn't I endure their shenanigans with good grace? But no, I . . . I lacked the capacity. Plus I couldn't help notice they were both wearing wedding rings. Still, who knows? Maybe they're happily remarried now and living in a fortified bunker someplace, pushing that big ole thing called life together for the long haul.

It took nearly six hours to fix the bus. This ate up my whole day—not that I had anything else on the docket. At last, I hopped in the bus and began the drive across town to pick up Gavin and Oliver. I was a few minutes away from the school when I caught the smell of burnt maple syrup coming from the back of the bus. Radiator fluid was pissing out of the heater. How had the mechanics taken six hours and *not* fixed that?

I carried on, fuming. Oliver and Gavin were waiting on the schoolyard grass.

"Hop in," I told them. "We're going to be a while."

I radioed in a Code Yellow. Dispatch said a mobile mechanic would be sent. When I told the boys what had happened and explained that it meant we'd be late getting home, Oliver was okay with it.

"We can just hang," he said loosely.

When he chose to be, Oliver could be laid-back. His most common response to any statement was a laconic, "I hear you." Ask him about his evening plans and his standard reply was, "I'll probably chill." At these times he possessed the easygoing, unperturbed manner of a California beach bum.

"Good day at school?" I asked.

"Yep . . . I'd say that's just about right." He gave a catlike stretch. "That's just about the size of it. Hey," he asked, "do you have a hot tub?"

"I have a *tub*-tub," I said. "I can fill it with hot water."

"I thought you were the type of guy who'd have a hot tub."

"Really?"

"Yeah, a hot tub and a fat wallet and a big house. A big shot."

I searched Oliver's face for signs that he was screwing with me. But the kid was being sincere.

"I drive a bus, Oliver. Bus drivers aren't exactly high rollers."

He mulled this over, then went on another tangent. Like most boys, Oliver got bored easily. Our conversations could veer into new terrain quite abruptly.

"Hey, you know two people I find very attractive?" he said. "One is Brad Pitt and the other is Angelina Jolie. If she ever dumps Brad I'd go to Hollywood and date her. After three dates I'd ask her to marry me. You could come visit us."

"That's a nice offer. Thanks."

"Brad's very handsome, too. If I were a girl I'd marry him."

But then Oliver's eyes dropped to the floor. A shiver rippled through him.

"What's the matter?"

Oliver raised his eyes and spoke fearfully. "Are the cops going to arrest me?"

It took a moment for me to understand the root of his anxiety. "Do you mean . . . for wanting to date Angelina Jolie?"

He nodded worriedly, stage-whispering: "I'm only thirteen."

I'd come to learn that Oliver lived in near-constant fear of being sent to juvenile detention, or "juvie" as he called it. Someone must have painted a hellish picture of such places— he seemed to believe that any infraction could get him sent there, from spitting on the sidewalk to chewing gum in class to the harmless and unconvictable crime of fantasizing about dating a Hollywood star.

"They won't send you to jail for that, Oliver."

Relief washed over him. "I don't think I could make it in juvie."

We decided to wait outside on the grass for the bus mechanic. Gavin picked the final tenacious leaves off a sapling planted in the schoolyard. The sun was bright but the day wasn't warm. I couldn't let the boys stay out for too long or they'd catch colds.

"Hey, Craig," said Oliver. "Guess what, dude?"

This, I would learn, was Oliver's all-time favourite conversational opening. With most people this phrase is followed by information of a linear nature, like: "Guess what? I'm getting married." But Oliver was fond of posing this question without anything at all to follow up with; this would lead to a long period where he wracked his brain for something to say, settling on gems like: "Hey, guess what? If you had a thousand dollars you could buy a Lamborghini."

"What, dude?" I said, happy that we were already at the "dude" point in our relationship.

Fifteen seconds went by.

"If you were my age, I could totally hook you up with a girlfriend."

I smiled. "That would be great, Oliver. Too bad I'm so old and ugly, huh?"

"Yeah, too bad."

The mechanic showed up. He fiddled around with the radiator, replaced a burst hose. Five minutes later we were on the road. I dropped the boys off at their homes; another driver had covered my high school drop-offs. I drove back to my neighbourhood and parked behind the abandoned house again. And that is when I hatched my plan. It was not a good one. I've never been renowned for my plans. But it was simplicity itself, and I felt sure it could not fail.

I would stake out my own bus and catch those foul vandals in the act. Yes. A sound decision.

Half an hour later I was hunkered down in the weed-tangled backyard of the abandoned house. The fence, though missing the odd slat, acted as a blind, shielding my presence from anyone in the alley. I had a water bottle and a few sandwiches and a lawn chair and some blankets for when the night's chill set in. I was loaded for bear. The vandals would meet their Waterloo at my hands.

For each of us there are moments in life that inevitably lead to the contemplation of the pitifulness of one's existence. This was such a moment. It was a Friday night. I was a grown man. I should not have been spending my evening in the yard of a condemned house, eating peanut butter sandwiches and dreaming of revenge. A man my age should have had hobbies, causes, a partner to tell him what an idiot he was being. I had none of those things. I didn't have many friends in the city, either, although I did keep in touch with a few of my old library co-workers; we'd get together and rehash "the ficus incident." Otherwise, I was socially inert. It didn't bother me much. I had good friends; they just lived in other places. And I've always been comfortable with solitude. Which was fortunate, because I was alone a lot. And now I had my obsessions to freely indulge.

Because I had time to kill, I imagined a conversation: what if a friend called me up to see what I was up to that night?

ME: Booked solid, amigo. I'll be sitting in a ratty lawnchair in the backyard of a ramshackle house waiting for vandals to attack my bus—at which point I will strike a blow for decency!

FRIEND: I seeeeee . . . what's your timing on that?

ME: Deep into the night, I'd imagine. If they don't come before ten o'clock, I'll sleep in the bus.

FRIEND: In the bus, you say . . .

ME: These scumbags attack under the cover of darkness, expecting the shadows to protect them. Nosirree! I'll be in the bus all night, in all probability.

FRIEND: All night, you say . . .

I sat in that yard for hours. Dogs barked in the adjacent field. I heard the sharp crack of a baseball bat from the ball diamond. The sounds of normal people leading fruitful lives. Once or twice I gathered up my possessions, struck by the ridiculousness of my endeavour . . . only to sit down again. A few times I caught the echo of footsteps in the alley, which sent a powerful wave of adrenaline through me—but each time, it was only joggers or dog walkers. I fell to brooding. What if it wasn't kids who had vandalized the bus—what if *adults* had been the culprits? I envisioned a neighbourhood watch group gathered in a dank basement, muttering, "Special needs? Oh no-no-*no*, we don't need that element on our streets. Time to send that driver a message."

Night fell. Mosquitoes began to suck out my blood and enthusiasm. But I knew that if I left the bus unattended for

even a split-second, those youthful louts would attack. I just
knew it. So.

Sleeping in a school bus is not comfortable, and a wheel-
chair-equipped bus is even less so. Having made a nest of
blankets, I lay on the floor sideways with my feet touching
the fire extinguisher. It was cold. I should have brought a
toque. I pictured tomorrow's breathless newspaper head-
line: VAGRANT FOUND FROZEN TO DEATH IN SCHOOL BUS!
Followed by an update the next day: BUS DRIVER MIS-
IDENTIFIED AS VAGRANT PERISHES IN BUS TWO MINUTES
FROM OWN HOME!

The night settled around the bus. From my spot on the
floor I could see a spider's web spanning one of the windows.
At the heart of the moonlit web sat the spider: small and
shiny, a drop of molten lead. The moon travelled a slow orbit
across the window glass. My mind travelled its own orbits.

From the start of the year, Jake's father had welcomed
me into his house. One afternoon early in the school year,
the door had swung open and Calvin had beckoned me in
when I brought Jake home. None of the other parents had
done anything like that. So when I stepped inside their home
those first couple of times, I could not have anticipated that
I would, in short order, become a gear in that unit's engine.
A family like Jake's had many cogs: doctors and aides and
resource workers and grief counsellors and others whose job
it is to ease the pain, and facilitate the transition back to the

kind of precarious normalcy that follows terrible upheaval. I was happy to be a part of that adaption process—it had been a while since I'd felt vital to anyone in any way.

It had struck me that most people's lives unfold through a constant process of recalibration. Things happen, often unexpectedly, and a person's life adjusts to account for them. I understood that Jake and his family were undergoing a drastic recalibration. A truck had slewed down their street one evening, and everything, absolutely *everything*, had changed.

Lost: a mother, a wife, a protector and anchor. Her presence lingered in that house. A blown up portrait of her dominated the front room. The licence plate of Calvin's new minivan read: SOULMTE. She was there in the stacks of books beside the television with titles such as *Good Grief: A Constructive Approach to the Problem of Loss*. She was everywhere and yet she was indisputably gone.

One day not long after we'd met, Calvin said, "If I could, I'd ask God to bring her back and take me in her place."

And I thought: What if my own mother had died suddenly when I was Jake's age? How would my father have managed? Never mind the emotional devastation—my father had never done the simple tasks of bagging lunches or cooking dinner or nursing my brother and me when we had to take a sick day off school. He would have floundered under the weight of day-to-day tasks he'd never been accountable for. Was Calvin floundering? Yeah, sure. But he was a tough, capable guy. Most days Calvin had it locked down, but every so often he would appear exhausted, his eyes bruised and haunted.

Our morning pickup time was 7:50. If the garage door didn't begin to rise until 7:55 or so, I could bet it had been a rough morning. On those days Jake was often withdrawn and morose; he'd been in "a row" with his father.

"He's got that teenage angst," Calvin was fond of saying.

Theirs was a loving if occasionally volatile relationship, as those between fathers and teenaged sons can be. Jake would say, "Dad's my best friend." And Calvin said Jake was the strongest person he'd ever known.

"The boy is made of sterner stuff," he'd say. But Calvin refused to let Jake feel sorry for himself or live in self-imposed isolation—this often lay at the root of their ruckuses.

"Dad tells me I need to get out more," was Jake's frequent lament. "Be more independent."

It was a rough situation, but one that would have been no different if Jake's mother was still alive. Jake was smart and charismatic, in a distinctly British way. He had a wild imagination and a talent for telling stories. But he didn't always push himself to share his intelligence and passion with others. He was a homebody, whereas Calvin was a dervish of action—he taught karate, dabbled in acting (he has since landed an ongoing role in a much-lauded cable drama), and had a wide circle of friends. He wanted the same for his son. *So, you've got CP*, Calvin's thinking went—*So what! Okay, you can't get around as easily as other boys. Doesn't mean you have to sit on your duff all day long, squirrelling yourself away in your room!*

Jake's mother had been less forceful, I was told. She was happy to have Jake hang around. They went for walks, read and watched television together. Surely she had wanted the same things that Calvin did: for her son to gain independence and pursue interesting work, to have a social network of peers and eventually a family of his own. But she was willing to let him figure that out in his own time.

I think Calvin had let a dismal prospect creep into his thoughts: he envisioned Jake living in the basement at forty, his only connection to the world a fibre-optic Internet cable. No egg should stay in the nest too long, he might have thought. But that put an awful lot of pressure on Jake to be outgoing, forever pushing outside his comfort zone. And while most teenagers are anomalies, Jake was a paradox: simultaneously the oldest and youngest person I'd ever met. In so many ways he was older than his sixteen years. There was his body, for a start. I'd catch glimpses of his legs through the vents in his tear-away pants, or his chest and arms when he readjusted in his wheelchair. He had so many scars: shallow trenches carved with tiny fish-gill pleats where sutures once held the lips of incisions together—lips through which tubes had been inserted to reinflate his lung, perhaps, or through which a good deal of his spleen had been removed.

Come Christmas, Jake would have Botox injected into his hips; this would allow for improved movement and ease some of his chronic pain. "Chronic" was a chilling word when applied to teenagers: aren't they too young to feel pain chronically? But that was Jake's reality. The following summer he would have steel rods inserted on either side of his spine to correct scoliosis-like symptoms.

I found myself thinking about the pain in Jake's body with an anatomical fierceness. Pick any square inch of it and calculate how often its pain receptors had been activated, the nervous system overtaxed. What Jake felt in that square inch would far exceed all the physical trauma I'd experienced in my life, and I was twice his age. I thought about the scars and the Botox and the divot in his lung where a puncture had transfixed it. The walnut of his spleen, his traumatized heart that kept on beating. I thought about those crucial imperfections within his cerebellum that made his body the way it was. How hypoxia, or lack of oxygen to his brain during birth, had shorted out a few critical connections.

As Jake once put it himself: "A million trains hurtle out of my brain with messages for my body, but they keep crashing into each other so the messages never get there."

But the ways in which Jake was older than his years influenced the ways in which he was simultaneously younger. His world was small and controlled. His home care aide helped him get ready in the morning. I took him to school. His in-class aide shadowed him throughout the school day. I drove him home, where his aide was waiting. Together, we formed a twenty-four-hour cycle of oversight. He was rarely alone, and the majority of his interactions were with the adults entrusted with his care.

"Once I got cross at my mother and father and wanted to run away," Jake once told me. "The front door was unlocked but I couldn't make it down the stairs. I couldn't open the garage door; the opener was out of reach. You see, Craig? I can't do much when I'm angry. I can't fight back or hit anybody. Usually when I am angry I get frustrated and start to cry."

As a result of his controlled world, Jake didn't go out much on his own. He would get the odd invite from school chums— or, as was becoming common, Calvin would take it upon himself to ring up Jake's buddies and make plans for them.

"Dad, don't!" Jake would say, mortified. Though he'd also admit, "I have more adult friends than I do my own age."

What are typical sixteen-year-olds up to? Getting driver's licences. Sneaking bottles of schnapps out of their folks' liquor cabinet. Playing sports. Dating. Bonding.

Jake couldn't drive. None of his friends' houses or cars were wheelchair accessible. He couldn't play sports. His mother had been killed by a drunk driver so he had no interest in boozing. He was crazy about girls, a new crush every week, but he didn't think any of them would want to date a guy in a wheelchair. His email address was "crazywheelchairdude"—like a lot of teenagers, he defined himself by a single physical characteristic. For me it had been my weight. But at least I'd had the option of losing a few pounds.

Everybody at his school knew and liked Jake but that didn't help his social aspirations. This was partly because it was physically problematic to include Jake in teenager activities; who was going to drag his wheelchair out of a muck hole when it got bogged down on the way to a bush party? And it was partly because—either through natural inclination or as a function of his shielded upbringing—his enthusiasms were often in keeping with those of a younger boy. Jake remained innocent even as his contemporaries were studiously abandoning that quality. He didn't question authority. He was respectful. His pop culture favourites skewed young: he was fond of Monty Python and *Homestar Runner* while others his age had moved on to more racy or violent material. Jake still liked *Thomas the Tank Engine*, something that must have made him seem quaint and perhaps a little weird to his fellow teens.

None of this was Jake's fault—his maturation had simply been different. He was as smart as anyone, smarter in many cases, but lacked that indefinable *cool*. He was too earnest and trusting, and he didn't fit any of the tidy teenager boxes: He wasn't a jock, a keener, a skid, a brain, a goth, a techie, or even a geek. And some of the elements that defined him—his wheelchair, the fact that he rode my bus—put him outside of many people's comfort zone. It would have taken an extraordinarily understanding sixteen-year-old to spend a lot of time with Jake. And outside of Hallmark Channel movies, those people are really hard to find.

I lay in the bus, torso bent round the raised latticework. My toes were going numb. What in God's name was I doing? It was three o'clock in the morning. The vandals were in bed snuggled up with their teddies. Ah, well. There was something peaceful about being in the bus.

"When my wife fell pregnant with Jake she had toxemia," Calvin had told me without prompting one day. "Severe high blood pressure. Since she was so ill from it, the doctors took Jake out via emergency cesarean section. So he was born nine-and-a-half weeks early. They really didn't expect him to survive. In fact the day he was born the midwife said, 'Listen, you've got to understand: your son is very, very poorly. If you want to have him christened I suggest you do it now, this morning, in the hospital.'

"Well, obviously he made it over that hurdle. Then at three days old there was a buildup of carbon dioxide in his bloodstream. We all exhale it, but there's no way of medically extracting it from the blood. So again he was facing death. The midwife said: 'When you're ready, come up to the incubation unit and I'll take him out so you can cuddle him goodbye.' It took a while to build up the courage and when I got up there—fantastic moment in my life—the midwife said he'd shown slight improvement. From that instant Jake went skyward. He just touched five pounds at seven-and-a-half months old. But my wife noticed he wasn't doing what a baby was supposed to. Not even sitting up. At twelve-and-a-half months the doctors confirmed he had cerebral palsy."

Calvin told me that his family had moved to Canada in hopes of a better life. And then one evening, Jake and his mom were out for a walk and a drunk driver tore apart the fragile fabric of their existence. How can a person process that, I wondered? And why hadn't awful things happened to the drunk in the Durango? Why couldn't he have been the one who skipped the curb, hit a light pole, launched himself through the windshield and smashed his skull open? *Fair.* Except fair had nothing to do with it. Instead, that driver lived under house arrest and was allowed out to watch his daughter's soccer games.

How must it have been for Calvin, knowing that the man who had killed his wife and critically injured his son was living just down the block? Calvin could drive past the man's house; he may have spotted the bastard in his garage, tinkering away on something to while away those hours under confinement. I got the sense that Calvin had been a hellion in his youth. His wife had managed to tame him, but the feral outlines still lurked: a coiled tension in his shoulders, a certain hooded aspect to his eyes. But his wife was gone now, and the man who had stolen her was within striking distance. I wondered whether the impulse ever came to Calvin in the sleepless hours of night: to get up, dress in dark clothing, find something heavy—a bat, the tire jack in the back of his pickup—stroll down the road through the pooled glow of the streetlights, find the man's house, lift the gate latch, steal into the backyard and scratch oh-so lightly on the back door, mimicking the sound of an animal seeking entrance . . . and then just *wait*.

Lying in my bus looking at the stars, I thought about how you can see all people as instruments guided by . . . fate? Karma? Yes, guided instruments pursuing our own discrete vectors. Most times we pass one another harmlessly. Sometimes we meet and it's magic. Other times we smash headlong into each other and it hurts like hell. Such events are random, sure, but speed is key: the more out of control you are, the more likely you'll achieve lethal velocity. I came to suspect that navigating through one's life at a conscientious speed, playing it safe and doing the right things and looking out for your fellow humans was no assurance of safety—because maybe you'd still get hit by a drunk in a Dodge Durango when out for a pleasant evening amble. Or maybe you wouldn't.

Unfair, unforgivable. These were the words my mind settled around. Yet, I asked: unfair according to *who*? Where was the scale to measure any of it—and of what value was such a scale in a world that so often appeared to hold no balance at all? The more I thought about it, the more I couldn't grasp it. Most of us were raised to believe that good things happen to good people, and wickedness is punished. But there comes a day when you realize this is a lie—just something your parents said to set you on the good path. Bad things happen to good people for no sensible reason at all. Bad people die happy in their beds. It happens every day, every minute of every hour.

For years, I didn't want to believe this conclusion—it's an assault on one's childlike sense of how the world ought to function. But the universe is chaotic; you will never impose order or logic upon it. This *should not* happen. So why does it happen? Only because it does. All the time, it does. As the clock ticked towards dawn in the dark and cold bus, I found myself accepting this.

As I write this now, years after that night, I still believe it is better to pursue the good, and to do good for others. This is what I will teach my own child. I'll tell him all those things my folks told me, even though they are lies. One privilege of childhood is to exist with that clean understanding of the world. I will let my child cling to a pure sense of fairness for a while. What could it hurt, really?

When the sun began to rise, I gathered my belongings and walked home. And before the next week began, I called the nearby public school and worked out an arrangement to park my bus in their lot.

9.

Some drivers ran their buses the way feudal lords ruled their fiefdoms, with an iron fist. Nothing made them happier than to glance at the riot mirror and see row upon row of tight-lipped students with their hands folded neatly in their laps. They relished tomb-like silence, as if they were delivering mannequins to a department store. I substituted on a few routes like that. It was eerie, that quiet. And the kids were ridiculously happy to get the slightest leeway.

"Wait," one kid said, "You mean I can drink my juice box *on the bus?*"

"Sure, go ahead. Just throw it out when you're done."

The kid beamed. "You are so cool!"

You're darn right I'm cool, kid! Drink that juice box, and hey—if you're feeling peckish, eat a granola bar too!

The rules on my own bus were more lax. If Oliver were to let a curse word slip every so often? Eh. The odd gum wrapper not thrown into the trash box at the back of the bus? Let it slide. But I made it known I was granting privileges, not according rights. In my previous roles as camp counsellor, classroom aide, librarian—I'd worked with kids a lot over the years—my objective had always been to treat those under my wing with respect; I'd allow minor infractions, hoping my charges would self-correct with gentle encouragement. Sometimes this backfired, but it was the method that worked best for me. Of course, it also reflected my distaste for being in charge. I didn't want to be the wet blanket. The scold. Better to be the laconic, laid-back, chill dude. Do what the rhythms of the earth and sea tell you to do, dudes and dud-ettes. Consult the I Ching. Gather the karmic threads of the universe and don't let me harsh your mellow. All of this to say that I was a terrible boss—or the best boss in the whole world, depending on your outlook.

I also didn't want to be driving a mausoleum; I wanted the kids to feel free to engage with each other and with me. And as they got used to me over time, those kids really did *talk*. About movies and sports and music and television and friendship and love and families and a million other topics. Mainly, though, the kids told stories. Their imaginations were astonishingly unbridled. And their stories were instructive—a window into their worlds and dreams. Every so often they broke my heart.

—

Let's start with Nadja.

She was the bus's social butterfly. Every day she would climb on board and say: "Good morning, Craig." Her voice had a tendency to rise at the end of every sentence, as if those final words were tethered to helium balloons.

"By the way," she usually asked, "how was your evening?"

By the way was one of her two pet expressions.

"All right. How was yours?"

"Actually, I had a dinner party."

Actually was the second of those pet expressions.

"And actually, it was very nice."

Nadja was forever attending dinner parties hosted by various aunties and uncles. Or so she said. Most of the kids presented me with a picture of their lives that was more . . . well, *lively*, than the reality. No harm in that. And Nadja did have a dozen or more relatives peppered around the city, so it was conceivable that she was out at parties every night. But according to Nadja, those same relatives had a preposterously high mortality rate. She'd fill me in on the details of their disaster-plagued existences every morning.

"My auntie? She had a nephew and he got very sick and . . . by the way, he died."

Over the course of the year, Nadja would go on to tell forty or more stories that ended in the same grisly, matter-of-fact manner. Car crashes and medical mishaps, airborne calamities and natural disasters. Her poor uncles and aunties and nephews and nieces were dying in terrible ways at a staggering clip. I was shocked they were holding so many dinner parties; they should have been holding wakes. I began to suspect that "by the way, so-and-so died" was Nadja's way of concluding a story that she could find no satisfactory means to end. Or perhaps she craved the outpouring of sympathy I felt compelled to provide. But as the months wore on and the death toll shot through the roof, I became considerably less sympathetic.

"My uncle had two daughters, Craig? And they were flying in a plane over the mountains? And it was very nice ... by the way, they died."

"All of them, Nadja? In a plane?"

"Yes."

"When was this?"

"Actually, it was last week. Isn't it sad?"

"Funny, I never heard of a plane crash. You'd think it would have made the papers."

"It's so *sad*, isn't it?"

"Nadja my dear, that's the way the ole cookie crumbles."

Nadja's stories often took off on fantastical orbits that defied the laws of nature—like the one about an epically fecund lass of Nadja's acquaintance.

"She's a little fat," Nadja told me. "But that's because, actually, she's pregnant? She has a lot of children. Ten."

I said, "Ten kids? That is a lot."

Nadja amended this number. "Ten thousand."

"Ten *thousand* children?"

"Yes."

"Holy shit!" Oliver cried from the back of the bus.

"Hey," I warned him. "Language, buster."

"She has ten thousand kids," Nadja went on primly. "All girls."

"Holy schizz!"

Oliver and I had recently settled on *schizz* as an acceptable substitute for "shit." I was already regretting it.

"And do you know how many husbands, Craig?"

"I couldn't even guess."

"Nine thousand."

"Holy hell's ass!" Oliver cried.

———

Oliver . . . oh, Oliver.

Oliver's stories, too, often took the shape of elaborate, reality-defying falsehoods. They were not so much lies as M.C. Escher-like masterpieces in which crazed helixes of untruths spiralled to half-sketched vanishing points; they were Babels of misinformation that defied all laws of physics, biology and common sense, and threatened to topple under the weight of their own audacious creation. At first I wondered whether I should indulge these outrageous deceits. Shouldn't I call him out? Wouldn't his teachers and parents do so? But Oliver was such a good-humoured liar that it was hard to call him one—he was more of a tall-tale teller, that wild-eyed character who bursts into the tavern in a fantasy novel with swashbuckling stories about orcs and trolls in faraway lands. Oliver's lies were thrilling in their monstrousness, cobbled together out of vague untruths and absurd leaps of imagination, often buttressed with whatever he happened to spy around him—he made up some of his best stories on the fly. And he told them with an absence of rancour and so much riotous dick-swinging panache that to deny the kid what was so obviously his calling struck me as an act of cruelty.

One morning Oliver showed me a photo on his cellphone. In it, he lounged on the hood of a yellow Porsche. He'd probably snapped the shot in a mall parking lot.

"Nice," I said. "Is that your car?"

I could see the gears winding in his head. A second ago, he'd merely been showing off a car he'd opportunistically taken a photo beside. But now I'd put the bug in his ear, intimating that I did not find the notion of a penniless thirteen-year-old owning a luxury roadster inconceivable—and you could see him thinking: *Why not?*

"Yeah," he said with a casual sniff, "I bought it this weekend."

"Oh. How much?"

Oliver narrowed his eyes, judging the depths of my credulity.

"A hundred bucks?"

"That's a good deal."

"Yeah, well, I haggled him down."

Usually Oliver didn't start the day off with such a whopper. He preferred to wade in gradually, testing the waters. Often he'd kick the morning off with a little white lie, such as: "I drank a nice big mug of java to get my day started."

He hadn't, of course. I'd be surprised if he'd ever tasted a sip of coffee. It was probably something he'd heard his mom or dad or someone in the line at the coffee shop say. But if this lie squeaked past, he'd forge into bolder territory.

"I'm going to join a gym today. But I've already got a well-developed upper body."

Oliver wasn't going to join a gym. His upper body was undeveloped—partly as a result of Fragile X, but more because boys his age weren't renowned for their rippling torsos. After coming to understand Oliver's ways, I was able to track the germination of his stories. One morning we passed a guy carrying a TV out to his pickup. Five minutes later Oliver said, "Me and my buddy Joey caught this guy stealing a TV yesterday."

"Yeah?"

"He was just walking down the road with it."

"How did you know it wasn't his own TV?"

"You could just tell."

"So what did you do?"

Oliver didn't speak for a while.

"You see those woods over there?" he said finally, pointing to a copse of trees skirting the roadside. "We chased him in there."

"What were you and Joey doing so far from home?"

Oliver ignored this. "The cops never found him."

"I didn't know they were looking."

"Yeah, he's probably dead."

Oliver was also the king of the non sequitor. His skill was breathtaking. Once, Vincent and I were talking about the local hockey team. Feeling left out, Oliver blurted: "The time I was born as a baby I weighed two-hundred and five pounds!"

"No you weeeeeren't," said Vincent. "You'd kill your mom."

Oliver said, "Seriously, I did."

"Kill her?" Jake said.

Undeterred, Oliver pressed on. "But hey, guess what? I've got tickets for tonight's hockey game."

"No you dooon't," Vincent said flatly.

"Yeah so!"

"Big whooooop," said Vincent. "I don't even liiiiike hockey."

"Oh YEAH?" Oliver said. "I'm gonna sneak into your house tonight and fart on your pillow!"

"Oh stop it," I said.

"*I WILL!*" Oliver shrieked. "I can lock-pick your door and everything!"

"Stop!" cried Jake, choking on laughter. "I can't *breathe!*"

Such outbursts were rare, though. Oliver's free-spirited fibs were usually delivered with an unassuming smile. *Take it or leave it, guys.* If you called him on one, he might cheerfully withdraw his claim or just stare out the window until the conversation moved to a new topic—that, or give an elaborate sigh, as if it was a Herculean labour to scatter pearls amongst such disbelieving swine. One afternoon he assumed a grave tone.

"I hate to tell you this, guys, but I have a big secret."

Big secrets were serious business on the bus. Everyone's ears pricked up.

Sombrely, Oliver said, "I smoke paper."

"You smoke cigarettes?" Jake said.

"No way. Those are bad for you. I smoke *paper*."

Mystified, Jake said, "How?"

"I tear a sheet into three strips, roll a strip up and—"

"Into a tube?" Jake said.

Oliver nodded emphatically. "A tube, yeah, and then I smoke it."

"Wait, so you don't put anything *in* the paper?" I said. "You don't fill it with anything? Just smoke the paper?"

"You bet. I light it up and suck it down."

A stranger might have wondered why Oliver put forward this particular fib. But by this time, I had come to know the boy; his reasoning was simple. Oliver bussed with high school students—he adored and looked up to Vincent, particularly—and he yearned to prove his street cred. So we were often treated to the fabricated confessions of a prepubescent bad boy who hadn't quite grasped the tenets of bad boyism.

"No big deal," Oliver said with a dismissive sniff. "So I smoke a little paper. So what?"

"That's a sophisticated attitude," Jake said. "How much do you smoke?"

"I smoke it all the time. Every day. I smoked a whole sheet for breakfast."

Jake said, "Nutritious."

"That could be a problem, man," I said gravely. "Paper is what's known as a gateway drug."

Oliver's brow crinkled. "Paper's not a drug."

"Well, no, but it's a habit," I pressed on. "And a habit can lead to worse habits. First it's only paper but next you're smoking big long birthday streamers."

"Then foolscap," Jake chimed in.

"Uh-huh," I said. "Then Bristol board. Then you're smoking any old thing you find wadded up in the wastebasket."

"Old Poooost-its," said Vincent.

"Before long you're begging people for paper so you can smoke it," Jake said. "It's a slippery slope."

"I only smoked paper once," Oliver said, backtracking now that the seriousness of his crime had been revealed to him—who knows, they might even send him to juvie for it. "One little puff. I didn't even suck in the smoke."

"I've eaten paper," Vincent said.

"I ate a Caramilk wrapper once," Jake said.

"With the choooocolate still inside?"

"No," Jake said, laughing. "Separately."

We were all laughing by then. The conversation had spiralled out of control, as it often did when Oliver was at the helm.

"You can smoke peeeyote," Vincent said. "I've eaten braaass rivets and aaaants."

We all agreed we'd eaten ants, everyone except Nadja: "Actually, I'd never eat ants. They are disgusting." And we agreed we'd eaten spiders, too, without knowing. According to Vincent, they liked to crawl into your mouth as you slept.

"I saw a guy come around the corner smoking a Caramilk wrapper!" Oliver hollered, and the bus broke into laughter again.

But of all Oliver's fantastical creations, none was so vivid as his best friend in the entire world, Joey. Joey appeared the way Batman does: whenever Oliver felt overmastered or marginalized, he would flash the Joey Signal into the sky and summon his best buddy, consummate confidante and ass-kicker—Joey, No Last Name Given.

"Joey could beat the schizz out of everyone on this bus!" he'd say. Or: "My best friend Joey, if you mess with him you will get your butt *beat*. He'll smack you up quicker than you can float a boat."

Should any of us ask for examples of Joey's legendary ass-kickery, Oliver was only too happy to oblige.

"Joey beat the schizz out of a ninth grader," he said excitedly one afternoon.

"How old is this Joey?" Jake wanted to know.

"He's twenty!"

Of course, trying to tell Oliver that a twenty-year-old beating up a ninth grader was less the mark of a tough guy than a child abuser was a waste of time. And anyway, we all knew Joey didn't exist.

"Nobody better mess with me," Oliver said, "or I'll tell Joey. And when he finds out he's gonna say, 'If they're messing with

Oliver, they will have to talk to my two friends.'" With stagey showmanship, Oliver kissed his right bicep. "'Thunder.'" Then he kissed his left bicep. "'And Gus.'"

Nothing sums up the nature of Oliver's wholly original comic genius better than this: It wasn't that Joey, the ultimate badass, might name his arms. Nor was it that he'd name one of them "Thunder."

It was the fact that he'd name the other one "Gus."

We all loved Oliver. He could be maddening, sure, and he had a hair-trigger and was sometimes hurtful (almost always accidentally so), but he was *ours* and we were fiercely protective of him. We all needed protecting sometimes, but perhaps Oliver most of all.

——

And then there was Gavin.

Gavin and I rapidly established a closed information loop, just the two of us—our own communication system. I imagine Gavin had similar systems with his parents and siblings and teachers.

It took a little while to establish the loop and work the bugs out. The initial hurdle was eye contact. Not a fan of it, was Gavin. But as the days wore on and autumn deepened, and Gavin got more comfortable, our eyes would touch fleetingly. He had these deep-pool eyes that actually *did* sparkle.

Gavin rarely spoke, and when he did, it was just the odd word. On November 13—I wrote the date in my notebook—the sky went grey over the Rockies and snow began to fall. It came down in airy balls that looked like fertilizer pellets as they piled up along the bus's rubber insulation strips.

"Snowstorm," Gavin said.

Gavin liked his routines, his folks and teachers told me. He liked it best when everything in his world was ordered and predictable. So when I found I had done something he enjoyed, I made sure to do it again, every day at the same time. For example, when I finished strapping down Jake's wheelchair for the afternoon run I would turn to Gavin— who sat in the same seat every day—give his shoulder a light squeeze and say, "Gavver!" Or in the mornings, when we were at the high school and I was lowering the wheelchair lift for Jake, I'd crouch under Gavin's window, tucking myself out of sight, then pop up like a jack-in-the-box. "Gavver!" Most days Gavin would smile bemusedly and cover his eyes as if to say, *Oh, brother.* Other times he would stare right past me at something else that had captured his attention. But I sensed he enjoyed these moments, and I kept them up all year.

Another routine that *I* loved was our serenades.

When we arrived at the middle school every morning, Oliver would leap out of his seat and charge into the school-yard. Gavin could be more reluctant. He'd gaze at the mill-ing kids as if readying himself for the ordeal of existing amongst them. So to get him moving I'd sing in a warbly basso profundo. I am a terrible singer. It was, I am sure, a chore for the boy to endure it. I chose familiar songs but warped the lyrics. For example, I'd do a take on the Police's "Roxanne."

Gaaaaa-vin! You'd don't have to wear the parka tonight;
Walk the streets for chocolate—you don't care if it's dark
*   or if it's white.*
Gaaaaa-vin! You don't have to put on the night-light;
You don't have to put on the niiiight-light, you don't have
*   to put on the niiight-aaah-light, you don't have to put*
*   on the night-LIGHT, yaaaaa . . .*

Or maybe I'd go with a few lines of "Mandy," by Barry Manilow.

Ooohhh Gavin, you came and you got on the bus, yeah
But now you must go to school, ohh Gavin,
Well you slapped me and stopped me from speeding
But now the school bells are pealing, ohh Gavin . . .

Michael Jackson's "Billie Jean" topped the charts for a few days (*Gavvy-Gav is not my rider, he's just a boy who won't get oooff of the bus . . .*) or "Ticket to Ride" by the Beatles (*Gav's got a ticket to ri-hide, oooh Gav's got a ticket to ri-HI-hide, Gav's got a ticket to ride—but not no more!*)

After scant moments of this torture Gavin would get up, waving his arms in a shushing gesture, and hop off. The schoolyard might hold its perils, but nothing was as bad as having to listen to his bus driver's awful caterwauling.

—

And: Vincent.

At seventeen years of age, Vincent was the oldest student on the bus. He sat directly behind me, often dominating the small percentage of my attention that wasn't focused on the road. He spun stories as diverse as "Magic Town," "The Immortal," "Time Cops," and "Future World." His stories were populated by warriors and sorcerers, rogue cops and cyborgs. When he said he was working on a story, I came to understand it was in much the same way Oliver worked on his lies—ie: he was working on it *currently*, on the fly.

"The main character's name is Beeeeell . . . Biiiiiillaaaa . . ." he would say, stretching his vowels as he searched for a name to settle on. ". . . *Bill*."

"So his name is Bill?" I'd ask.

"Yes. Definitely Bill. No, Huuuugo. No, Claire. A girl."

"Okay, got it. What's her story?"

"She's immoooortal. She's been in every war from the Cruuusades to Iraq."

"What are her powers?" I would ask, because Vincent's characters *always* had powers.

"She's got super strength, super inteeeelligence, she's got a machine that can make an infinite amount of money. And she's a lesbian. Claire and her girlfriend vowed to be with oooone another until the end of tiiiime. They fight crime together. Do you want to know what her costume is?"

"Of course."

"Claire wears a goalie mask autographed by Terry Saaawchuk and her old Naaazi uniform. But she's not a Nazi. She was just confused during that time of her life."

Vincent didn't shy away from racy subject matter. He was at that age. Hormones blazing. Take the following story, which unfolded over a breathless week on the bus—"The Hooker Rebellion."

"There are three laaaady hookers. Their names are Stella, Mina, and Jinn. They have M61 Vulcan Gaaaatling guns. And photon grenades."

"Okay, cool. Who are they fighting?"

"Oppression."

"From who?"

"Aaaanti-feminists."

Vincent's characters tended to start as normal people, but he'd lard on so many exceptional powers that a man who started as a mild-mannered janitor would morph into a super-strong vigilante crime-fighter with cybernetic limbs who happened to mop floors in his downtime. Sometimes he'd write down a story and hand it to me. He knew I'd made my living as a writer before hitting the skids; he wanted my opinion "as a pro," as he said—bless him. One of those stories was called "Magic Town"; after reading it I asked if he would let me reprint it if I ever wrote my own book about driving the bus. Sure, Vincent said.

All rights reserved to the original author:

There is no light or dark only magic.
I set upon a hole in the ground.
MAGIC TOWN HELP CENTRE.
I walked up to the building. This sign above the
entrance said: "Est 1396."
"Welcome," said the girl. "I'm Lily may I help you?"
"Yes. A date?"
"Okay."
"Nice. Oh, and where do I get a guild licence?"
"Fourth floor."
Up to the office and approved.
Then Lily said, "Ready Duck Bo?"
"Yes, but how do you know my name?"
"Remember me?"
"Lily." I hugged her.
Then I kissed her.
"Wow," she said in a slightly expaserated voice.
"I know," I said with a malishous grin.
Then after she took me on a tour of Magic Town.
THE END?

"That's a fantastic story," I told him. "Duck Bo—coolest
character name *ever*."

Many writers could learn a lesson in conciseness from
Vincent. He wasn't one for fluff. And yes, his stories reflected

the adolescent views of a much younger boy—but you know what? Plenty of guys in my own high school had been functionally illiterate; they couldn't have *read* what Vincent had written, let alone have written such a story themselves. And those guys hadn't been in special classes, like Vincent was. I wasn't fighting the idea that Vincent had to be in those classes by that point, but I had begun to compare the capabilities of the kids on my bus against the other kids at school—and I often found that my group measured up. Did Vincent misspell "exasperated" and "malicious"? Yeah, but he wasn't far off the correct spelling, he understood the usage, and he had those five-dollar words in his arsenal, which was more than could be said for some of the burnouts walking the hallways of his own school. *I'd* have misspelled those words at his age.

If there was a sameness to Vincent's stories, if his protagonists had a Steven-Seagalish infallibility that stole an element of risk from their journeys—"I'm no good at emooootions," Vincent freely admitted—his tales held a sweetness similar to that of their teller. Take "The Immortal," which ended with Claire at her girlfriend's bedside as she died.

"She's saaaad but she's not sad, too," Vincent said of Claire, "because she knows her girlfriend lived a good life and died haaaappy."

I said, "You don't give yourself enough credit, Vincent. You can be very good at emotions."

Finally, we had Jake.

He was the most serious creative mind on the bus, and the most intense young writer I'd ever met. My own interest in writing had started in high school—but had consisted of noodling away at English assignments, writing a few stories because I wouldn't have passed the grade otherwise. I didn't throw myself full-bore into writing until I was in my mid-twenties. Jake was hammering away at it by sixteen. The writing bug hadn't simply bitten him; it had sunk its fangs deep into his neck, piggybacking everywhere he went.

As we drove the sleepy thorough-fares and cul-de-sacs that made up my route, Jake regaled me with stories. At the beginning of the year they were Space Operas: waylaid starship explorers trying to find their way home or a ragtag crew of humans, aliens, and cybernetic helpmates staring down a dire intergalactic threat. Jake's stories were similar in two ways. One, they always ended with the explorers safely home or the threat vanquished. Two, they featured a young male character with telekinesis, or the ability to move objects with his mind, without any reliance on his body. This character wasn't the dashing commander or the surly starship mechanic who, as Jake might have said, "keeps this clanking bucket of bolts afloat!"—but he was always involved in the mission's success in some minor yet essential way.

Then, a couple of months into the year Jake said he was working on a manuscript—an honest to goodness *novel*—tentatively titled "Mystery Academy." By the end of the year it would be 140 single-spaced pages long—an impressive feat at any age. Jake had written a book. At *sixteen*.

"You need to have drama and fear and high incident," he told me in October, once we had begun to get comfortable with each other. "And you've got to keep the tension at a fever pitch before laying off. And—and, *and!*—you've got to have comedy. Your comic foil. And romance. But not drippy."

Jake envisioned "Mystery Academy" as a series, six or seven or even eight novels: an epic on the scale of Harry Potter or *Lord of the Rings*. They would be books full of derring-do, cliffhanger endings, love powerful enough to melt binding chains, dramatic revelations, life and death and lots of belly laughs. He worked on it most nights. In the mornings he'd give me the latest update.

"Ninety pages now!"

"One hundred and two!"

"Big night—one hundred and twelve!"

"Good news and bad news, Craig. Bad news: *waaay* too much social studies homework last night. Good news: I still wrote a page on my novel!"

The hero of his novel was once again a boy with telekinetic powers. Jake gave me hell when I mixed up telekinesis and telepathy.

"Telepathic means someone can read another person's mind. Telekinetic means he can move objects *with* his mind. How many times do I have to tell you?"

Obviously, I would take these opportunities to irritate him further.

"Oh, so your main character has one of those machines like in *Star Trek*, the one that zaps Captain Kirk and Bones and Scotty from the *Enterprise* down to the surface of a planet?"

"Arghh! No, that's *teleportation!* It's all different! Captain *Kirk?* You're so old."

"Okay, okay, let me get this straight. So you're saying"—I shook my head at the inconceivability—"you're saying that your main character operates some kind of long-distance communication system that enables him to send messages to people hundreds of miles awa—"

"That's, that's, oh what do they call it . . . *telegraphy!* He doesn't have a telegraph. *Nobody* has a telegraph anymore. They're in museums. Stop taking the piss, Craig. I mean it."

"Okay, okay. But let me get this straight—"

"*Seriously,*" Jake said in an ominous tone.

"Got it," I relented. "Telekinesis. Moves objects with his mind. Like Charles Xavier, right?"

"Right."

"But your character's not in a wheelchair, like Xavier?"

"No. His legs work fine."

The main characters in Jake's novel were battling a dark force. Something huge and unknowable that Jake dreamt one night—his villain had literally come to him in a nightmare. When I asked him to tell me about this baddie, Jake couldn't articulate anything beyond a vaporous, seething hate: the hatred his villain exuded, and the hatred Jake felt towards his own creation.

"I hate him so much," he'd say heatedly. "He's so awful!"

I was never able to discern if Jake kept his villain vague on purpose—one of the rules of writing is to leave the worst things in the shadows and let readers use their imaginations—or if he did not *want* to approach his villain head-on, to give it a name, a face. If he had, Jake might have found that he recognized that monster. It might have lived in the same suburb, a few scant blocks away. Its driveway might have had a Rorschach stain where a busted-up Dodge Durango had leaked a pint of oil over the macadam.

Jake's telekinetic hero harboured a secret—a past event unknown to even the hero himself. Somehow, in some way, he was responsible for his mother's death.

I made no mention of the parallels to Jake's own life. It's entirely possible that Jake *knew* he was working through big issues with that book. That's the great and powerful thing about fiction. You can make up worlds to answer the questions the real world is incapable of answering. Jake rarely asked for advice, but I remember telling him this:

"It's okay to use your own life in fiction. You don't have to make things up whole cloth. Your own life has value, right? The unique things you've experienced. All you have to do is go back to those galvanic moments in your past and write from there. Take everything you've felt and thought and put it on the page."

But there was no need to tell Jake that. He was a writer. He already knew.

——

Over and over, I'd hear the kids' stories. Repeated, embellished, glossed, the same terrain covered and re-covered until a well-worn path had been carved. I could recite them from memory. I knew when the moments of high drama would arrive, and knew my own role—when to respond with an appropriately encouraging *oooh* or *aaah*. But I never got bored of those tales. They were like a book or film for which you had long fondness; you'd take it down off the shelf or pop it in the VHS player (Jake was right—I *was* old!) and read a few pages or watch a few minutes, and unfailingly, it filled you with deep satisfaction. They were a safety blanket of sorts to the kids, and that's what they became to me, too. I felt snug and happy within the parameters of their tales.

We tell ourselves stories in order to live. Another, wiser writer said that. But after hearing these kids' stories, I was left thinking: do we not also tell stories to live vicariously in ways we cannot?

Nadja's tales of never-ending dinner parties were those of a young girl who lived in a modest condominium complex and yearned for a taste of the glamour glimpsed in the fashion magazines she toted in her Hannah Montana backpack.

Or consider Oliver's best friend Joey: erstwhile protector, he-man, namer of biceps. Not a boy with a condition typified by low muscle tone, a boy who crouched in the bus to avoid the attention of neighbourhood bullies.

Vincent's heroes were blessed with superior intellects and chiselled musculatures. None were awkward, hormonal teenagers with cumbersome physiques.

Jake's hero—who could move objects with the power of his exceptional mind—was breathed into life by a boy trapped inside his own diminishing body.

Were these fictional characters or polar selves?

I am no different. I've never written myself—my true self—into one of my novels. I may have pillaged aspects of my existence—moments of fleeting grace, snapshots from the past—but who wants to read about a red-haired schlub whose life has been comparatively uneventful and privileged? So I write about characters struggling to surmount circumstances I've never faced, calling upon a strain of willpower and inner strength I have never possessed, not for one minute.

We all want a bigger life, don't we? Even those who've scaled mountain peaks must dream of ascending to the clouds when they close their eyes to sleep. The inability to find complete satisfaction is woven to the heart of the human condition. We all feel it—that witching hour thought: *Isn't there more than this?* In fiction, we can vicariously achieve everything that eludes us. Attain a heightened nobility. Be our best selves: best friend, best partner, best parent. We can put our proximal selves in the service of some grand Good, sling-shotting ourselves into wondrous adventures where we always do the right thing, show the courage we can't always display in life, kiss the boy or girl of our dreams and live happily ever after.

That is why such narratives never go out of style—because if you do it just right, others will want to live in the world you've created. They want to breathe outside of themselves for a while before returning to the real world, where the intensities are muted and dreams don't always come true.

Jake and the other kids conjured new lives into existence every day—any life they wished. They had already discovered something it takes some storytellers half a lifetime to figure out: tell the stories that lie nearest to your heart. That way, they're not really fabrications at all. They're hopeful truths.

10.

Halloween arrived. I decided to do it up big time. I rented an unzipped open-front jumpsuit (not just open-*throat*; this bad boy unzipped down to the navel) from a costume shop. Wig, sideburns, gold-frame sunglasses. Elvis, baby! The jumpsuit chafed my nipples mightily. Damn you, rayon! The wig itched my scalp so god-awfully you'd think it was lined with fibreglass insulation. And of course the bus needed its own costume. I spent the night before the big day gussying it up with orange and black crepe-paper streamers.

When I reached the bus the next morning, a spider's web was strung between the driver's side window and the mirror. This had been the case most mornings for the past few weeks. I had no clue where the spider was. I knocked the web down with the broom during my inspection—I felt bad, but the wind would tear it apart as I drove anyway.

"Elvis!" Jake said when I showed up at his house. "I thought you died."

"Whaa-hah, oh-ho, yeah, yeah, yeah-yeah-yeah," I crooned in my best/worst Elvis voice. "Everyone thinks ole Elvis P died on a toilet. Not true, buddy-roo. Elvis was selling home insurance in Reno. Now I'm driving a bus-a-reeno."

"What's that on your head?"

"Ma hair!" I said, mock-affronted.

"Looks like a dead skunk."

"What are you going as, man? It's Halloween."

Jake smiled. "I'm going as 'Guy in Wheelchair.' It's totally *method*. Or meta. Or possibly both."

We picked up Vincent, who hadn't bothered to dress up either. High-schoolers! Not a drop of Halloween spirit. The wig's coarse lining was making my skull sweat; it really did feel like I had a dead skunk strapped to my head.

"Aaaahm Elvis!" I said. "But in your bus driver's body. Y'see, when I died—"

"I thought you didn't die," Jake cut in. "You were selling insurance."

"Don't interrupt *Elvis!*" I thundered. "Now when I died, I made sure Colonel Tom Parker saved my brain in a pickle jar. Like Hitler's brain, yeah?"

"Nobody saved Hitler's braaaain," said Vincent.

"What's with the interruptions? Now last night ole Colonel Tom bonked your bus driver on his fat head, took his useless little pea brain out and put my robust Memphian brain in."

Vincent said, "Your brain in a pickle jar? What a cheapskaaate."

"Cheesecake?" I said hopefully.

"*Cheapskate.*"

At the next stop we picked up Oliver. Jake asked him what costume he was wearing.

"I'm not dressed as anything. But I am a vampire. For real," Oliver said.

"Whoa, nelly!" I said. "Elvis don't want no bloodsuckers on thissee here bus."

"I'm a vampire, too," said Jake.

"You can't be!" Oliver said. "You can't even walk."

"Who says vampires have to walk?" Jake challenged. "They can *float.*"

"Neither of you are vampires. That's physically impoooosible," said Vincent.

"Sure I am!" Oliver said cheerily. "I sucked that kid bone-dry."

"What kid are you talking about?" Jake asked, already chuckling.

"His blood tasted like cherries," Oliver said cryptically, then settled into silence before erupting with: "And at night I turn into an electric guitar!"

"You mean," Jake said, laughter beginning to overtake him, "instead of a bat?"

"Yeah! I turn into an electric guitar and float outside my friend's window."

The bus erupted in laughter. As it washed over him, Oliver's features fixed themselves into an expression of supreme satisfaction.

"Yeah," he said with studied nonchalance, "I knew you guys would get a kick out of that one. If I were a vampire I'd hardly kill anyone."

"That's noble of you," I said, my laughter subsiding.

"But if I was a werewolf I guess I'd eat everyone on this bus."

When I picked up Gavin, he tentatively raised my gold-rimmed sunglasses to make sure it was just his wacky ole driver. He covered his eyes with his hand as if to say: *I am SO embarrassed for you.*

After making my drop-offs, I radioed dispatch. The reply came back: *There's an elementary route that needs to be covered. Late bell. You interested?*

I'd covered the odd substitute route and, while they could be hit or miss, a little extra money was always welcome. I agreed to do it.

The dispatcher sounded shocked. "Well, okay then."

I soon discovered this was a rookie move. I had no idea that a *ton* of veteran special needs drivers begged off their routes on Halloween day. They came down with every minor complication under the sun: twenty-four-hour flus and food poisoning and temporary blindness and hysterical pregnancy—anything, anything *at all* to avoid those dreaded Halloween runs.

What could be so bad about Halloween? I wondered. It's the second-best holiday of the year, just behind Christmas. Kids *love* Halloween.

The answer was a painful lesson.

———

My first pickup on the sub route was a skeleton—or rather, a nine-year-old boy in a black leotard adorned with phosphorescent skeleton bones. He was joined at the next stop by a boy with the creepy face of an old man, courtesy of the latex mask he was wearing. A pair of princesses boarded after that. Their dresses were made out of flimsy material that resembled mosquito netting; moments after getting on one of them got her skirt trapped in the seat belt and it tore a few inches. This was a mind-melting catastrophe for the little princess.

"My dress!" she wailed wretchedly. "Stupid seat! My *dresssss!*"

"It's okay, you'll be fine." I had precious little experience calming princesses; she flipped her hand at me dismissively and said, "What do *you* know?"

While the princesses attended to this fashion disaster I drove to a nearby subdivision to pick up—surprise!—another princess. This one's name was Madison. The route report said she had asthma and ADHD; this struck me as a heartbreaking combination, the equivalent of a racehorse with a heart murmur. As she clambered aboard, it twigged: I *knew* Madison. Not personally, but by reputation. My heart jolted. Could it be—*the* Madison? Mythical creature of lore? Madison had acquired fabled status amongst the bus drivers on the southern end of the city. Legend had it that her energy levels were depthless; it was rumoured that in the event of a power outage you could simply ask Madison to hop on a treadmill wired to the electric grid and give her a

Snickers bar; she would generate enough electricity to power ten city blocks.

"She's a little hyper today," her mother told me with a forced smile.

We drove on. Madison sat quietly—suspiciously so—with her hands folded. She was like that little fellow in a chop-socky movie standing motionless to one side while the fight raged around him: you just *knew* he was going to leap into action before long, and when he did things were bound to get gruesome.

The final rider was a boy who hadn't dressed up as anything. This earned him the round derision of the skeleton, Dorian Gray, and the trio of princesses.

"He's *nothing*," said the princess with the ripped dress. "He's *boooooring*."

"That's not very nice," I said in defence of the poor boy.

The princess merely shrugged, gripping the edge of her seat and bouncing madly. Madison took this moment to break her silence, going off like a miniature Vesuvius.

"Bloo-bloo-BLOO!" she sang at a lung-rupturing pitch. "BA-ba-DA-DAAAA, DOO-DOOD-A-LOOOOT-DOOOT-DOOT-Ah-*DOOOOOOO*!"

I asked her royal highness to pipe down. The Princess was *not* amused, nor did she stop. In fact, Madison got the other kids to join in. My ears were ringing by the time my rolling madhouse reached the school's parking lot. The kids boiled out of the doors and began tear-assing around the playground.

I killed a few hours and returned to pick them up just before noon. Six or seven buses lined the curb. Heather, a driver I knew a little, came over to shoot the breeze. Heather and I both picked up kids at the high school. Three weeks ago she'd been in an accident at a traffic bottleneck. She'd slammed her bus into a pickup truck. Thankfully no kids had been on board.

"I got suspended," she told me with a desultory smirk. "Two weeks."

I already knew this but played dumb. "Suspended?"

"Yeah. Get this: I tested positive for THC. Can you believe it?"

Tetrahydrocannabinol. The primary psychoactive catalyst in the cannabis plant. As a matter of fact, yeah, I could believe it. Heather was *clearly* a pothead. Her clothes smelled aggressively of the devil's weed. Heather was such a colossal pothead that her urine probably had roach and stem floating in it. Such a pothead that if you were to position an extremely sensitive microphone beside said urine, it would likely emit the faint but unmistakable strains of "No Woman, No Cry."

All of which was fine. I had my own vices. But there was Heather copping bafflement to a positive test on a substance she inhaled only slightly less regularly than oxygen. It bothered me to have to play along, registering surprise at the completely logical/accurate test result.

"I've been eating a lot of poppy seeds," she said. "Muffins, bagels. That must be it."

Wouldn't that result in a positive test for opiates? Most pot-fanciers I knew were straightforward and even strident about their use. I could get behind that. So you smoke enough weed to reanimate Bob Marley—fine, own it. I'm almost certain that Heather's fondness for the sticky-icky hadn't been the cause of the accident, but as I recall, it was her second smash-up of the year. She probably shouldn't have been on the road.

"That must be it, Heather," I said nonetheless. "All those muffins."

I didn't hang out with many of the other drivers. The only one I talked to regularly was Audrey. She and I picked up at the middle school every afternoon; we'd get there twenty minutes early and chew the fat. Audrey was seventy. She'd been driving a bus forty-odd years. Her husband was sick; he stayed at home, resting in an oxygen tent. Audrey knitted a lot. The Kleenex box on her bus sat on a knitted doily. Her bus smelled of cinnamon; if anything, mine smelled slightly of boy's BO. Audrey's kids adored her. Two of her grandchildren had autism and rode a special needs bus. Audrey had never been in a bus accident. She was not a self-deluding pothead. I liked Audrey a whole lot.

Heather wasn't the norm. Neither was Audrey. They sat at opposing poles of the spectrum; the rest of us existed somewhere in the middle. But there were more Audreys than Heathers, thank goodness.

When the bell rang I said goodbye to Heather and returned to my bus. The school doors burst open. Gaggles of witches and superheroes, pirates and fairies, and a metric ton of princesses swarmed the playground. They fled across the grass slipping on their capes, tiaras knocked askew, magic wands crunched under the frantic trampling of feet. One boy dressed as Batman fell; I watched several of his classmates run over his back, squashing him into the muck. But instead of bleating the boy was smiling as if pleased with his self-sacrifice—*I'm just like Batman!* he may have been thinking. *Go, good citizens of Gotham, flee to safety across the broad bridge of my back! May your boots remain forever unmuddied!*

To my dismay I realized the children had been sent on their way with bags of candy. As they filed onto the bus I was further disheartened to note that most of the bags were empty, filled with shed wrappers. What kind of vile social experiment were the teachers administering here? They may as well have sent the kids out with a stick of dynamite in either hand, their hair lit on fire to ignite the wicks. I pictured the teachers in their lounge, chortling merrily.

TEACHER 1: I said, Go ahead kids—eat it all! Every bite of sugary goodness. Hoover it down your gullets! What do I care? You're the bus driver's problem now.

TEACHER 2: Oh Phyllis, you're perfectly *awful!*

TEACHER 1: Ah, screw the bus driver. He's a sub. A *scab*. I'll never set eyes on him again. He can go to the devil for all I care.

(Teachers lift their coffee mugs in a toast.)
TEACHERS: Screw the bus drivers!

A second scene flashed through my mind: the driver of the route I was covering sitting on a La-Z-Boy, nursing whatever bunko affliction he'd begged off with—Uncontrollable Flatulence Disorder or Exploding Head Syndrome, who knew—cracking a beer in front of the TV and cackling.

I beheld a bus packed with sugar-tweakers. It was as bleak a hellscape as I'd ever seen. These were the same kids who had ridden with me scant hours ago, but their costumes were now in various stages of disintegration: grass-stained and ripped and pulled out of shape, the sleeves rucked up so they could "Breathe—ohmygodohmyGOD it's so *HOT!*" They were all blue- or red-tongued from the sweets they'd eaten. Gobs of multicoloured goo were glued to the edges of their mouths. They had that over-sugared look, sticky-fingered and untamed.

And then there was the hyperactive asthmatic princess, the mythical Madison . . . Her hands and mouth were dyed with crystalized orange residue. Her dress was shredded to ribbons, as if she'd gotten into a scrape with a honey badger— and *won*.

Simply getting the kids belted in was an ordeal to inspire any number of debilitating neuroses. As soon as I had got a few kids battened down and turned my back to help the others, the first batch popped their belts and began to bop around shrieking, insisting they switch seats. I ended up tightening their seat belts to allow limited mobility—all except Madison, who seemed intent on tearing her shoulders out of joint to get free. She strained against her belt and arched her neck with such insistence that I was convinced her skeleton wished to flee her skin.

The urge to radio dispatch was powerful. "Mayday, mayday! I've got a busload of kids whacked out of their trees on Halloween candy! We're coming in hot! Check that—we're going down in flames!"

But by now I knew that if I did so, all I'd get was a knowing chuckle from dispatch, followed by: "Yeah, that's pretty standard. Go with God, new fish."

Feeling helpless, I settled on the seldom effective "Escalating Hey" technique.

"Hey guys, okay, okay, let's settle down . . . hey now, settle down . . . hey! Hey! *HEEEEY!*"

Somehow—divine intercession, perhaps?—we managed to get on the road. Within a minute I began to hear the ominous crinkle of candy wrappers.

"No candy!" I pleaded. "Wait until you're home. Candy tastes ten times better when you're at home. This is a scientific *fact!*"

We must have pulled over a dozen times so I could rebuckle seat belts, let the kids switch seats, prise candy out of tightly clenched fists and issue increasingly confounded warnings.

"I am warning you, so help me God."

"God helps those who help themselves," said the kid who hadn't dressed in a costume—a good comeback, I had to admit.

The entire bus was bug-eyed and weird. The kids licked their lips compulsively, often bursting into wild laughter. What had the teachers been feeding these kids? Cotton candy drenched in maple syrup? Hi-C and Sour Patch Kids, the grade-school equivalent of an eight ball?

"Can I eat a pudding?" Madison asked innocently.

"No pudding!" I barked. "We hit a bump and you'll be wearing it."

"Bloo-blap-*blooey!*" she pouted. "But I never got to eat it all day."

"Get used to it. Life's full of disappointments."

"Do you like being a HandiBus driver?" she asked.

"You guys would rather it was a *candy* bus, I bet," I said inanely.

"Candy bus!" Madison said, latching onto the idea. "That means you'd be a candy driver. That means we'd have to eat your smelly big toe! Eeww! Do you have a wife, mister bus driver?"

"Nope."

"I know somebody you could date."

I had to smile. "Is that right?"

"Her name is Jen," Madison said, ticking Jen's qualities off on her fingers. "One, she's pretty. Two, she's smart. Three, she's my homeschool teacher. Four, she's pretty. Five, she has two sons. Five *again*, she is single."

Something went *psssht!* The pressurized hiss of a soda can opening? To my misfortune, I ignored that sound—leading to "The Great Red Bull Halloween Freakout."

Now I am not claiming that Red Bull is an instrument of the devil. In the right hands it is a fine and worthy product. Among its devotees are a great many cramming college students, long haul truckers, and reluctant parachutists. But the combination of Red Bull, elementary-school children, and an enclosed moving space encourages ghastly results.

Soon an empty silver-and-red can rolled lazily down the aisle, coming to rest against my seat. Oh God. Mother of *GOD.* I could not have been any more terrified had it been a live grenade. I rapidly churned through the Five Stages of Grief.

Denial: *This is not happening! This can't be happening!*
Anger: *Who gave that to them? Who gives that stuff to kids?*
Bargaining: *Please, bus gods, be merciful to your humble servant.*
Depression: *Oh God! Why did I accept this route? I'm doomed.*
Acceptance: *Buck up and roll with it, buttercup.*

I pulled over in time to see one of the princesses chugging the dregs of a second can. The kids had been passing them around secretly. Twelve prepubescent eyes quivered in twelve sockets, peering intently at me.

"Uh-oh spaghetti-ooooo," Madison said, ooh so softly.

The panicky voice of an army drill sergeant began to shriek in my head.

Go, dogface! Go, go, go! Hightail it! Now, before they hit full caffeination and tear you limb from limb!

I pulled back onto the road in a desperate frame of mind. The kids bopped and wriggled in their seats with such force I was sure they'd tear the floor bolts out. To hell with using the engine—I could harness them to the bumper, put the bus in neutral, and let them pull it like a dogsled. Madison could probably do it all on her own, setting a Guinness World Record.

My charges began to sing: a devilish, lowing howl. There weren't many words to be parsed out of the noise; I was certain all six of them were singing different songs. They threw themselves around as the caffeine blitzed through their redhot neural clusters.

I laughed. What else could I do? I laughed and sang my own tune—a song my old instructor Don had written.

"If you want to be rich, be rich! Hahahaha-hoHO! *If you want to dream then dream with all your might!"*

You could call it a hellish journey, and for stretches it certainly was. But as we drove through the darkening day, through suburbs in readiness for Halloween—houses with jack-o'-lanterns burning on stoops and garbage-bag ghosts suspended from tree boughs—with the kids singing in their tattered costumes, I began to feel there was also a thimbleful of pure joy to be wrung out of the experience.

I dropped the kids off one by one. They charged off the bus hollering like banshees, spinning in whirligigging dervishes or dancing jag-legged jigs on the sidewalk. The looks their folks gave me were more forgiving than angry.

Madison was the last drop-off. At her stop she held a pair of mittens out to me. It took me a moment to register that she wanted me to help put them on.

"Hold your hands out, Madison," I said tiredly, tugging them over her orange-stained fingers. "Stay still and stop wriggling, for Pete's sake."

"Will you drive us tomorrow?"

"Tomorrow's the weekend, Madison."

"Oh pooh."

She stepped off the bus. Her princess costume was rucked up, showing a slice of bare skin up her back. I saw a scar there and was reminded that most of the children I drove had suffered in some way. *An insult*, is the medical term. A critical insult to the body or mind, sometimes both. You can try to forget that, I realized, but this job had a way of reminding you.

Madison stopped. She was looking at something. She pointed one mittened hand. "It's a spider."

She was right. A small black spider sat on the bus's side mirror. The same one, I guessed, that had been building the webs I'd torn down every morning the past few weeks. It must have been living in the housing behind the mirror, coming out at night to string its web.

"Its home is behind the mirror," I told her.

She frowned. "A spider shouldn't live there. It should live in a tree."

I wasn't sure that a tree was a spider's proper element but I was too exhausted to argue. Madison reached for it. She was too short.

"Give me a lift."

The spider couldn't be poisonous, could it? It was a common everyday spider. I'd seen others just like it. I held the princess under the armpits and lifted her up. She tried to pluck the spider off the mirror but it skittered away and she ended up knocking it off the glass. It rappelled to the ground on an invisible gossamer skein. I lowered Madison. She knelt and fussed with the spider until it climbed onto her mitten.

"Yay! We're friends."

She went over to the tree in her front yard and put the spider on the trunk. She waved at me and sat on her front steps and took off the mittens I'd just put on. She pulled her pudding cup out of her backpack and tore the top off. She ate it daintily with a plastic spoon, gazing at the tree. There was something ineffably . . . beautiful, I guess, and sweet and a little melancholic about a ten-year-old hyperactive asthmatic girl in a shredded princess costume eating banana pudding on the steps of a cookie-cutter suburban home, watching her new friend the spider. Huh.

Madison's mother opened the door. Madison waved at me again, spoon clutched in her hand. I waved to her, to her mother, and headed home. I was dog-tired—the result of mental fatigue more than heavy lifting. I parked the bus and jammed the "anti-theft pin"—the steel bolt attached to a loop of steel cable, *très* high-tech—into the emergency door, locking it. I armed the motion-sensor alarm and secured the wheelchair door with a padlock.

The sky was ashy as I walked across the field towards home. Early stars pricked the sky. Children's giddy voices floated over the rooftops as they made their way from house to house. A father guided a pair of youthful vampires in matching red snowpants down the sidewalk. Cold-blooded as vamps could be, evidently their fathers still made them bundle up for trick-or-treating.

A word came to me: *normal*. It had been a gloriously normal day. I'd woken up. Driven the bus. Got those kids home safely. Small achievements, sure, but no less tangible for that. As normal a day as might transpire for anyone my age. I'd been useful. It had been a while since I'd felt vitally so.

Simple tasks, I told myself. Complete them as best you're able. Repeat day after day. Before long, you're normal.

WINTER

From

"THE SEEKERS,"

an unpublished novel

The van rumbled down the road. Nondescript, grey, its windows blacked out. It could have been carrying anything. But the driver was young, his hair clipped military style. He wore a thick leather belt with a holster. In the holster was a pistol.

The van had four seats. Ripley sat in the one closest to the back. Two boys sat in the seats ahead of her. They had been marched aboard an hour ago by a pair of unsmiling guards. The boy directly in front of her was a shrimp with hair so blond it looked white. The boy sitting to her left was bigger and more muscular, with a large head and a mushroom-cloud of brown hair. That boy stared straight ahead, his eyes fixed on the back of the driver's head. The small boy fell asleep as soon as the van had started to move. He slept peacefully, his breath fogging the glass.

They hit a bump. The small boy woke with a snort, rubbed his eyes and reached over to touch the big boy's shoulder. He then threw one arm over the back of his seat and craned his head around to stare directly at Ripley. His eyes were a frosty blue. Ripley noted the hairline wrinkles at the corners of his mouth and eyes—they made him look older than his age, which she figured to be fifteen or so.

"How are they hanging, sister?"

The boy grinned, showing a lot of teeth. Ripley resisted the urge to roll her eyes. That was exactly what the boy wanted. Her years in institutions had taught her that the best tactic was to match fire with fire.

"Low and lazy, little guy."

The boy's grin faded, then returned at an even higher wattage.

"Little guy, huh?" he said breezily. "Ouch. But it's like they say. Big things come in small packages."

Ripley stared out the window, ignoring him. Fields rolled past, acre upon acre.

"I'm Oliver," the boy said.

"Congratulations," she said, still looking out the window.

"Hey," Oliver said. "You dropped something."

"What?"

"My jaw. You're so beautiful."

This time, Ripley couldn't help it. She rolled her eyes. Oliver leaned back, impressed with himself.

"Yeah," he said, "I thought you'd like that."

Now the big boy swivelled to face her. He had an open, gentle face with soft expressive eyes. His hands were huge, even bigger proportionately than the rest of him. Meathooks, thought Ripley. He could probably wring the juice out of a grapefruit with his bare hands.

"You honour us with your attention," Oliver said to his companion. "You going to introduce yourself, you big lug?"

The boy blinked slowly then faced back towards the driver.

"That is my trusty associate." Oliver hooked a thumb at the big boy. "He doesn't speak much. He does a lot of think-ing." He leaned in and spoke in a conspiratorial whisper. "You don't want to mess with him. But don't worry. Me and him are best buds."

Ripley sank back in her seat. The trees were thicken-ing along the road. Wherever they were going, it was in the middle of nowhere.

"You must have been pretty desperate, huh?" Oliver was observing her earnestly now. "To take the guy's offer, I mean. No disrespect. I was desperate, too. Juvie, man. It's not for me. I'm a bird. I got to fly free." He turned pensive. "I guess I shouldn't have stolen all that stuff, huh?"

"I guess not," she said.

"I've been thinking," he said. "Why us? You, me, this big ape over here. What's the connection?"

Ripley saw the driver's eyes tick to the rearview mirror, watching them in the reflection.

"We're all losers," Oliver said, answering his own ques-tion. "That must be it. It's the truth, right? Nobody wants us. We're the factory recalls. Charter members of The Island of Misfit Toys."

Oliver began to sing. "Nooooobody likes us, everybody hates us, we're going to the garden to eat worms. Biiiig fat juicy ones; long thin slimy ones; itsy-bitsy crawly-wawly wooooorms . . ."

The van pulled off the paved road onto a dirt one. The fir trees rose all around, a wall of green.

They rode for a long time in silence, hearing nothing but gravel bouncing off the sides of the van. Ripley put her chin on the back of Oliver's chair and watched through the windshield. At last, the trees peeled away. The van rolled into a flat expanse hidden in the middle of the woods. Ripley calculated that it must be at least a mile wide.

Buildings stood in the centre of the clearing. Structures made of metal and glass rose from the forest floor. The biggest was a jet-black pyramid. The compound was surrounded by a towering fence topped with coils of barbed wire.

Oliver let out a shivery breath. "Holy . . . schizz."

11.

The cold arrived early that year. The mercury dropped like a guillotine blade. One day it was minus eight and seasonal; the next day a cold front curled in from the Alaskan Pacific and down the Rockies. I woke up to minus thirty.

The alarm buzzed at 5:30 am. I rose groggily and fumbled my clothes on in the dark. Longjohns, tube socks followed by wool socks, long-sleeved shirt, hoodie, another hoodie, trousers. I tromped downstairs to the phone and called the bus company's automated service line to sign in for the morning route.

"This is the roll call line. Please leave your name and route number. Thank you and have a great day."

"Craig Davidson. Route 412."

Out the kitchen window, the view was like one of those establishing shots in John Carpenter's *The Thing*: a vista of clean arctic white. Snow piled heavily on rooftops, on cars, drifting thigh-high at the roadsides. I yanked on a toque. Boots. Magic gloves. Mittens overtop of the gloves. A parka. Then I waddled out the front door.

It was bone-snap cold. The kind of cold where the outer shell of your parka freezes instantly, making crinkly tinfoil noises as you walk. So cold that the mucous freezes in your nose and crimps your nostrils shut. The wind needled through tiny slits in my winterized armour, bringing up gooseflesh on the knobs of my spine. I trudged across the snow-draped fields to the bus. The sun was a sickle of crystalline orange spread across the earth's curve. My coffee was already frozen around the rim of my thermos cup. Smoke lifted from chimneys and the tailpipes of passing trucks, the vapour torn into ragged threads by the gusting wind.

I reached the elementary school, where I'd been parking the bus after it was vandalized. I knocked off the snow piled against the doors and wrenched them open just wide enough to slip through. The lot hadn't been plowed; snow was piled two feet deep in spots. There was a good chance the bus would be stuck. I sat behind the wheel. The seat was hard and bonelike. I cranked the key in the ignition.

Whrrrrrr-whirra-whr-r-r-r—r—r . . .

No surprise. It rarely fired on the first try. I gave it another go.

Whrrrrr-rrrihhrrr-pikka-pikka-pikka . . .

I thumped a mittened hand on the wheel.

"We'll be there when we can," dispatch said when I called in the Code Yellow. "We've got no-starts all over the map."

I waited inside the bus. The windows went opaque from the white clouds of breath puffing from my mouth. The day brightened. I stepped outside. A flock of masochistic birds were frozen in flight against the gunmetal sky. Some nutcase staggered along the unshovelled sidewalk wearing nothing but a sweater. He was walking a Scottish terrier wearing a tartan overcoat and doggie boots. The snow was so deep that the dog seemed to disappear into it—as though the man was holding a leash with nothing attached.

A while later, a mechanic showed up. He cracked the hood and said, "Yup. The same all over." Evidently it was so cold that the oil inside the crankcase had frozen into greasy black brick. The mechanic backed his van up to the bus. He popped the van's rear doors, revealing a bank of heavy-duty batteries wired into a cube the size of a concert speaker. He hooked up the booster cables and gunned the van's engine and signalled for me to twist the key and pump the gas pedal. After a few tries the engine rumbled to life. Once the bus was running, dispatch radioed to tell me to bring it into the yard; by then it was too late to pick up my kids, anyway.

Arriving at the yard, I was given grim news. My bus, trusty ole 3077, was being sent north to Fort McMurray, a township in dire need of units. I went down to the common room, where a mechanic with a face like a bowl of knuckles took the keys. He cocked his thumb, directing me to follow him into the yard. As soon as we got outside he pulled a thick cigar from his pocket and lit up. I inhaled its wet-fart smell as we crossed the yard to where my replacement bus was parked.

Unit 1456—ugh. Those four digits make me ill to this day. The dodgiest, saddest, rustiest, piece-a-crappiest bus in the entire fleet. It was rigged for three wheelchairs, meaning there weren't enough seats for my kids to sit on their own. Vincent weighed well over 200 pounds, and Gavin and Oliver had serious personal space issues. Gone was my beloved Q'Straint wheelchair system; in its place was the fussy strap-and-ratchet system that had nearly given my buzzcut instructor an aneurism.

I left the bus and stomped across the yard with rage smouldering in my chest. Had anyone taken a second to consider the needs of my kids before switching the bus? Three wheelchair spaces when there was only one wheelchair passenger. Four seats for six passengers. Plus this vehicle was *white*. A white school bus! It was unseemly. Who gave a rip about Fort McMurray? Bus 3077 was *ours*. The kids *loved* that bus. *I* loved that bus. And now they thought they could simply steal it away? We'd just see about that.

The mechanic was standing outside the common room puffing on his reeking cancer stick as I headed into the office.

"That thing stinks," I said as I shoved past him through a narrow doorway, the two of us so close our parkas rubbed together with a silky susurrus.

"You stink," the mechanic said. I had no retort to this.

I stood inside the office vestibule. The dispatch room lay

up a narrow flight of stairs. I took the steps two at a time, pogoing up the staircase—

I stopped. What was I doing? This was the ficus plant incident all over again, wasn't it? Was I still that immature? Was I going to quit over this—was I even going to *threaten* to quit and take the risk of being let go in order to keep the bus I preferred? Or was it better to buck up, deal with the situation and work towards getting a better bus in a more measured way?

If I quit, that was it. I wouldn't be driving those kids. The company would find another driver. There was nothing special about me. The kids might miss me for a while but they would get over it. Bus drivers came and went.

The vestibule door opened below me, ushering in a draft of cold air. Another driver mounted the stairs and stopped. I was blocking the stairwell.

"Going up or coming down?" she said.

"Coming down, thanks."

That afternoon I drove terrible, shuddery old 1456 to the high school. The wheelchair ramp rattled against the window so hard that I was certain the glass would shatter. Everything shook and wobbled—the bus was safe, but it sucked. I arrived a few minutes late. The kids were waiting outside in jeans and short-sleeved shirts. Were there other forms of life as unstintingly masochistic as the North American teenager, I mused? Piling onto the new bus, my kids noted the downgrade immediately.

"Where are all the seeeeats?" said Vincent.

"You'll have to buddy up," I said.

"I want to sit a-*lone*," said Nadja.

"And I'd like a banana split, but I can't have one right now. Only Jake gets his own seat, and that's the same one he sits in all day long."

With much grumbling, we hit the road. I assured the kids that I'd make a big stink with my bosses and get a new bus. And I carried through on the promise, badgering the dispatchers until they got sick of my complaints and assigned me a better unit, 1644. It was still white, and still not as good as 3077—you never really get over your first love, do you? But it had my cherished Q'Straint system, and enough seats for everyone.

12.

The cold persisted. The city was blanketed in an impenetrable layer of snow. One night I heard a sharp *bang* in my garage, loud as a gunshot. I flicked on the light and scanned the space, my breath sparkling whitely in the frigid air. Nothing seemed out of place. I pushed the garage door opener. Nothing happened. This was when I realized that the massive spring operating the door lift was broken—it was so cold that the metal had snapped clean in half. As I didn't have the funds to fix it, I parked my car in the driveway and plugged in the block heater.

Driving was tricky, and frequently a misery. The bus was rickety in the cold; the metal shrank slightly and the doors no longer met the frame flush, making everything rattle. Treacherous black ice lay beneath a scrim of powdery snow on the roadways. The bus was forever getting stuck in unplowed cul-de-sacs—thank goodness for kind suburbanites who pitched in to help me shovel it out. Late arrivals at school became routine. Jake and I would jockey his wheelchair into the school, he working the joystick control while I shouldered the heavy chair through the hampering snow.

As the cold snap stretched into its third week, the city's residents prayed for a chinook. One afternoon during this intolerable span, I pulled up at Jake's house. Calvin was waiting outside in a parka.

"Come on in, Craig. I want to show you something."

The warmth of the house was pleasant, almost narcotic. I heard the pop and crackle of a fire burning in another room. Boxes of medical supplies stamped ANDA MED were stacked next to the door. Beside these was a mechanical stair-lift that ferried Jake up to the second floor, following the wide sweep of the staircase. As we entered, Jake's sister Molly threw her arms around Jake's shoulders and hugged him tight.

"You're crushing me, Molly."

She said, "Your hair smells like a wet dog."

"Dad!" Jake protested.

"Molly, quit pestering your brother."

Here, I realized, was another odd facet of Jake's existence—his relationship with his sister. Under normal circumstances Jake, as the big brother, would have been pulling Molly's pigtails and locking her in the closet; instead it was his sister, eight years Jake's junior, who physically dominated him.

Calvin held up for my approval his newest purchase: a replica mask of the Predator, from the 80s Schwarzenegger film. The family had received an insurance settlement recently;

Calvin, a comic book buff, had also bought a replica gun from the Hellboy universe.

"It's retail therapy," he told me.

"Dad!" Jake squawked.

Molly was teasing Jake's snow-wet hair into spikes. Jake was powerless to stop her.

"Molly, I told you. Quit pestering your brother."

"I'm *styling* it."

Calvin shooed her away. "My son," he said to Jake. "Have you spoken to Craig about our idea?"

Jake dropped his head. "Not yet."

"Well, what's stopping you?"

Jake stared at his dad furiously. I got the sense he was being railroaded into something—something that Jake had probably told himself he'd say when he was good and ready. But Calvin was always pushing; he saw it as his fatherly duty to harry his son across thresholds he might otherwise avoid.

"Craig," Jake said haltingly, "would you like to go out sometime?"

Listening to his smooth British accent, I felt as though Jake had just invited me to the Duchess's Grand Cotillion Ball.

"You mean dinner and a movie?"

I meant this as a joke, but Jake said seriously, "Something like that. But if you're too busy . . ."

I suddenly saw that Jake was terrified I'd find some way to wriggle off the hook. He was giving me a loophole so that I could let him down easy.

I said, "Sounds like a plan, my man."

Jake's head came up. His eyes were wide and shocked. Maybe he'd expected me to say no—maybe he'd *wanted* me to say no.

"See?" Calvin said. "Ask a fair question, get a fair answer."

"Dad . . ."

Calvin clapped me on the back and ushered me to the front door. His voice found a lower octave.

"Listen, Craig, there's a provincial care form we can fill out that will pay you for your time with Jake. You'll get an hourly rate, a few dollars above minimum wage at least."

"Oh," I said, a bit stunned. "That's not necessary, Calvin."

"Well, think about it."

———

So began the unlikely saga of the washed-up writer and the unlucky young man in the wheelchair (which, of course, was not how we were viewed by others and not really how we viewed ourselves, except when we were sunk in corrosive moods).

Jake and I started to hang out away from the bus. I'd come over to the house on weekends and play board games with him, Molly, and a roving platoon of caregivers. Or we'd go out for lunch then catch a matinee—our "outings," as Jake called them. We went where he felt most safe, our destinations chosen by him so that they assuaged all logistical concerns—wheelchair accessibility, mainly.

At the movies we'd watch PG or PG-13 fare. I might have been able to sneak Jake into something a little more racy—well, not *sneak* (hard to do when one of us was in a wheelchair), but I could have appealed to the usher and got us in. But Jake had no interest in adult themes or scares. He preferred comedies and fantasies—movies with make-believe worlds similar to his novel-in-progress. For lunch we'd go to Boston Pizza or Moxie's, moderately priced and accessible places with pretty waitresses. Calvin would slip Jake a couple of twenties and loan me his wheelchair-accessible minivan. Sometimes we'd go to a shopping centre and mall-crawl. We could spend hours at that, goofing around.

"What if I buy you a hair weave from that kiosk, Craig?"

"Buy me a wig. I'll wear a wig."

Once, I threatened to push him into Bombay Company and tell everyone he was buying beaded throw pillows and honeydew-scented aromatherapy candles.

"That's okay," Jake said, shrugging. "I like those things."

"You know what?" I said. "So do I."

Our conversations tended towards silliness. We'd make up spontaneous stories populated by characters with names like Hummingbird Jones, Poodle McElroy, and Copperhead Mulvaney. We'd riff off each other, urging one another to higher levels of lunacy until we both broke into delighted gales of laughter and Jake was left whimpering, "No more . . . I can't breathe . . ."

Jake taught me a bunch of goofy games, such as one where

you give the plot of a make-believe TV show or movie and the other person has to guess the name.

"This is a show about a bunch of Canadians who drive around in a van helping out people in trouble."

"*Hoser Patrol?*"

"No, Craig. Try again."

"*Canucks in a Van?*"

"No."

"I give up."

"*The Eh Team!*"

A sixteen-year-old and his bus driver palling around— sometimes I'd step back and ask myself, was it a little weird? And the reassuring answer was: Sure, but people fall together in all sorts of odd ways. And the truth was, Jake and I got on like bandits. We were both pathologically incapable of being quiet so we were forever conjuring up new diversions and games to push the silence away. Was there a note of forced hilarity? Sure, sometimes; we both knew that if we let the silliness stop, more serious feelings might bubble to the surface. Jake didn't want that. So we settled upon a wilful avoidance of "Topics of Substance." On those few occasions I tried to steer the conversation towards an "Issue," Jake adroitly turned the ship around and steered us back to his preferred waters: Science fiction. Make believe. Avoidance of real life.

"Reality is highly overrated," he'd say. "I prefer fantasy."

———

My grandfather, a native Englishman, joined the British Air Force in World War II. He wanted to fly planes, but myopia prevented him from passing the eye exam. He became a navigator, a duty that suited his disposition. A careful and thoughtful man, my grandpa plotted his own life with the same precision as he did the vector of a DC10 bomber through German airspace.

He flew missions in shrapnel-studded skies, survived, counted his blessings and when the war ended he moved to Canada. He met my grandmother. They soon married. My grandparents built their own house. This amazes me. They dug the foundation, erected the frame, mortared the walls, laid down floors and tacked the carpet, nailed shingles, ran electricity and plumbing. Though only two generations removed from that, I myself can barely hammer a nail.

What I remember vividly are my grandfather's hands: massive, knobbed, knuckles big as marbles. He had a skin disorder that gave them a speckled appearance: deep tan and white, like the dappled hide of a palomino. He died of liver cancer. He was diagnosed, fought it, almost licked it. He had an operation and got measurably better. Just when we started to believe he'd beaten it, the cancer roared back and killed him.

The final months of his life, he stayed with us. My grandmother had already passed by then. My mother, a palliative care nurse, brought a wheelchair home from the hospital. He'd sit outside on the chair in chilly fall days with a blanket over his legs, looking like Winston Churchill minus the cigar.

In his last days he couldn't have weighed more than ninety pounds. His skin was a vein-webbed yellow, so thin that I could see the whiteness of bone at his temples. There was nothing left of his liver. What hadn't been cut out had been colonized by a trillion cancerous cells. He wore diapers. Mom encouraged him to go whenever he felt the need, but at this final humiliation Grandpa rebelled. The bathroom was seven footsteps away from his bed. To a man as sick as my grandfather, that was an enormous distance. That was *Pluto*. What struck me was how ruthlessly the illness scaled back my grandfather's range. At first he couldn't go outside without the chair. Then he couldn't climb the stairs. In the end he couldn't even make it to the toilet.

Mom brought a portable latrine into his bedroom. She couldn't lift Grandpa herself, so I helped move him. Mom unfastened his diapers. I saw that his body was destroyed. I was furious at Mom for involving me. But looking back I realize that she needed my muscle and nothing more, and that although she was a nurse and the procedure was familiar to her, she was in as much pain as my grandfather—just a different kind. In retrospect, I marvel at her strength. I hope I'll be able to do the same if I'm ever in that position.

My mother and I would slide our arms under Grandpa's arms. He refused to open his eyes. Perhaps he couldn't stand the sight of his own squandered body. Or he didn't want to see the mingled pity and dread in his grandson's eyes—or in the eyes of his daughter who he'd nuzzled and sang lullabies to all those years ago. We'd hoist him onto the latrine. I tried to be gentle but I knew it hurt him—still, he never registered a complaint. I saw my grandfather's penis. A shrunken mushroom cap in a thatch of tight grey curls. Neither Grandpa nor I wanted that—surely he'd seen my penis, bathing me or changing my Pampers as an infant, but that was comical. This wasn't funny at all. Sickness, I saw, reduces us, steals the dignity we've fought and clawed our whole lives to maintain.

My grandfather had flown flak-blistered skies over Dresden. He grew up hard and perhaps it was his fate to die that way, too. I wish like hell that it had been otherwise. The day he passed away, his daughter, my mother, wiped his bottom as he had wiped hers as a baby. His grandson helped him into the bed he'd shortly die in. All things come around.

From time to time while hanging out with Jake, I thought about my grandfather. The physically reduced life he experienced in his final days mirrored Jake's own day-to-day as a teenager. Jake's CP wasn't killing him the way cancer had taken my grandfather's life, but it had led to the same ruthless downscaling of his existence. Jake used to be able to walk. He used to be able to do lots of everyday tasks we take for granted. But the neurological connections in his mind were in a constant state of deterioration.

"I'll never go camping again," he said to me once. "You will never get a wheelchair into a forest." Sardonically, he added: "Too many of the world's most beautiful places aren't paved."

Sometimes we'd be heading out the door and he'd say, "Just a moment, I've got to brush my teeth"—then he would go into the bathroom where Molly or Calvin or his caregiver would do the brushing. He had difficulty wielding a knife and fork, so eating with Jake meant cutting his chicken cutlet or pizza slice. At home his cups had snap-on lids with flexible plastic straws. Sippy cups, essentially. He had a hard time raising a glass to his lips without spilling, so instead he would crane his head down and drink from the straw like an elegant bird dipping its beak to drink at a lagoon.

The first time I noticed things like this, well, I found it wrenching—especially knowing that Jake used to be able to do those things himself. But I got used to it. Calvin or Molly (or me, in time) cut Jake's meat, combed his hair and helped brush his teeth. His family performed these small intimacies with an offhand brusqueness that was touching. They weren't bothered by them and put little thought into the act; they were just habitual routines. I recognized these as the same kinds of intimacies that my mother and grandfather shared during the months my grandpa had spent at our house.

When I hung out with Jake myself, I found there were obvious differences in how I treated him compared to how I would have treated most kids. Some of these differences were small, some not-so-small. The small: if the waitress set his glass too far away, I'd nonchalantly move it closer so Jake could drink. Also small: at the movies we'd take the eleva-tor (I hadn't realized theatres had them) to the second floor, and sit at the very front where there were empty spots for wheelchairs—spots whose purpose I'd never even understood until then. I'd pour popcorn from our shared bag into a child's size box on Jake's lap. When he was thirsty I'd take the cup from the cup-holder and hold it up so he could wrap his lips around the straw. When the movie ended I'd brush the popcorn shrapnel off his wheelchair. The smallest intimacies, casually rendered.

During my driver training, our instructor had cautioned about students with special needs: "Only help as much as they ask." Jake knew he often needed help and, although he didn't welcome it outright, he consented to receiving aid. Sometimes this balancing act could get awkward, with me trying to anticipate his needs; I'd offer him a sip of cola at the movies and he'd whisper peevishly, "I just drank five minutes ago." I'd sit there thinking: *How do I know, dude? I've never had to guess when a buddy of mine might be thirsty.* I began to notice that the other kids on the bus helped Jake out in the tiniest ways, too. Gavin would reseat Jake's hat on his head if it got knocked askew. Nadja would put his water bottle back in his lap if it fell on the floor. Jake's collars were forever getting flipped up; Vincent would turn them down with infinite care, his huge fingers working so gently.

I also began to see that, as significant as Jake's physical debilitations were, things could have been much worse. One afternoon I was over playing board games with Jake when a young girl with cerebral palsy stopped by for a visit. Her

CP was so pronounced—and perhaps made worse by other neurological disorders—that she could not move. She lay in a recumbent wheelchair with her head elevated, her eyes looking to the side at nothing.

"Say hello to everyone," her caregiver said cheerfully. The girl did not, or could not, make any noise at all. "She says hello," her caregiver said in time. "She's so happy to be here."

The girl's body was curled into a fetal question mark. Medical pillows were arranged around her hips and shoulders to keep her comfortable or at least fixed in place. She shook constantly.

"I feel so sorry for her," Jake said, once she'd gone.

Intellectually speaking, Jake's mind was in perfect shape. His synaptic clusters glowed with ideas. He was in Grade 11, the appropriate grade for his age, and he was killing it. He may have been into obscure pop cultural phenomena, sure, but he could derive supreme satisfaction from books, movies, and TV. What's more, he understood how they worked: we'd be watching an episode of a television show and he'd say, "You see what happened there? That offhand thing he said? They're going to circle back to that. It will all hinge on that." And he'd be spot on. He would watch shows over and over, dissecting them to see how they worked dramatically and narratively. That was something I'd only just begun to do: taking apart my favourite books and films like a watch-maker, seeing what made them tick in hopes of improving my own writing. He grasped irony, sarcasm, double-meanings and the complex undercurrents of character development that I was convinced others his age wouldn't have discerned.

I thought: *He's sharp as a blade. He understands nuance. He's got one hell of a work ethic. Why can't he get exactly what he wants out of life?*

13.

The more time I spent with Jake that winter, the more I saw that he showed precious little interest in venturing outside his closed orbit. He also understood that with minimal coaxing he could keep a lot of people, me included, locked in that orbit with him. Jake obliged me to meet him at his level, which meant keeping things light at all times and avoiding talk of the "real" world. I wasn't always happy to do so, but I complied on account of Jake's history and what he'd been through. As a result, we went to the films and ate at the restaurants he chose. We played the games he wanted to play and held forth on the topics he selected. The minds of most teenagers travel on fixed trajectories, don't they? Was Jake really so different? I'd ask myself. But the self-imposed narrowness of his world was troubling in light of the one serious topic Jake did allow us to discuss: his lack of friends his own age.

Everyone liked Jake, including his classmates. There was precious little *not* to like. He was genuinely funny and smart and deferential and didn't take anything too seriously or feel sorry for himself. He set people at ease—as if he knew his condition inspired trepidation and had made it his goal to erase that. But there's a difference between liking somebody and spending a lot of time with them. Every so often Jake would talk excitedly about plans to go out for lunch or to the bookstore with friends, but those plans inevitably fell apart at the last minute. Who was breaking them, Jake or his friends? It was hard to say. Perhaps it was his friends, because their plans involved something Jake couldn't do: candlepin bowling, maybe a trip to the wave pool (Jake *could* do those activities, but at his own speed and not without help). Or was it Jake, because he got cold feet and preferred to remain in safe, known waters? He could have me come over and play board games or watch *The Holy Grail* for the umpteenth time.

Reflecting on it now, I think it may simply have been that Jake's experiences were so different from those of a typical teenager—his life followed a curve entirely its own. And his habit was to make people follow his curve instead of bending to meet theirs. He was more comfortable pushing his own interests, confident that if he pushed hard enough you would accept them. He preferred that to taking an interest in other people's pursuits. I could play silly games with him all afternoon, sure. But kids his own age might have been frustrated and bored by that.

As time went by, though, I began to harbour misgivings. Like his father, I wished I could motivate Jake to break away from his small world and try new things. But how would I accomplish that? Stop accepting his invitations? No more lunches, no more flicks? Stop hanging out with Jake, full stop? That would be manipulative, the equivalent of emotional blackmail. I couldn't imagine driving him on the bus if I did that—his bruised eyes staring at me in the riot mirror. Plus I'd be depriving myself of his company.

Still, more and more I sympathized with Calvin and came to share his worry: the prospect of Jake gradually isolating himself, shrinking into a world of his own interests and enthusiasms, shutting most of the world out.

———

"If he needs it, the pee bottle's in his backpack."

Calvin had said this to me the first time Jake and I went on an outing. I'd never considered how or when my friends went to the bathroom. Did I dig the bottle out of Jake's backpack and let him take it into the toilet and take care of things? Or was my role a little more involved?

Over the first little while, Jake made a point of drinking very little when we were out—and so it took me a while to register why he got peevish when I prodded him to drink his cola. But eventually, as the date for Jake's spinal surgery loomed, Calvin started to get on him about drinking more fluids and eating more to get his strength up. Finally, at the end of one particular day when we'd spent six or seven hours together, Jake finally broke.

"I need to go to the bathroom, Craig."

I shrugged, no biggie—though in truth I was flustered at the prospect. "Okay, sure. What would you like me to do?"

Please say just give me the bottle I can take it from there please say just give me the bottle I can take it from there—

"You're going to have to help."

"No problem. Just however you usually do it, okay?"

I'll never forget the care Jake took. He recognized that this was an unusual experience for me and calmly guided us both through the procedure.

"Unbutton my pants first."

Jake wore tear-away pants with buttons down the side. Warm-ups, I called them; the kind of pants basketball players wear on the bench before ripping them off with a dramatic flourish at the scorer's table. I made the nervous mistake of unbuttoning them all the way down to his ankles. His legs, I saw, were skinny as matchsticks. The hair on his kneecaps was worn down to stubble by the ceaseless friction of those nylon tear-aways rubbing against them.

Jake chuckled. "A little *too* far, Craig."

I refastened a few snaps. "Better?"

Jake nodded. "Now this might seem strange, but I'm wearing a diaper."

"That's not strange. Not at all."

The bottle was plastic. Hypoallergenic polyurethane with a spillproof cap. It seemed eminently suitable for the job.

"Now put the bottle between my legs."

"Like that?"

"It's . . . okay, okay. Good enough."

The wide mouth rubbed against his thighs. I tugged his pants down a bit further and helped him spread his legs. Jake's eyes were rolling back in his head slightly, his leg quivering with the dire need to urinate. I felt so bad that he'd held out this long, praying his father would come home.

"Now hold me inside it, please."

I did as he asked. Trying not to pinch him, to be gentle, but that's the thing about penises: everyone's particular about how theirs is handled. There's an art and a delicacy to it, and a lot of us only learn how to handle our own.

"All right, Jake? Nothing's pinching?"

"It's fine," he said, though his face was wrenched in pain.

He relieved himself. The bottle warmed in my hands. When he was nearly done Jake said: "You should have gotten toilet paper."

"Ag! Why didn't you tell me?"

"I'm sorry. Time was of the essence."

"I'm only kidding." We were in the kitchen. "I can reach the paper towels."

"Those will be fine."

He dabbed himself dry and together we tucked him back inside the diaper. I refastened the tabs. Nothing to it! Jake was relieved, as one can only be after a long-delayed pee. We went back to watching TV. But I thought: Would one of his

friends be willing to do that? Would I have been okay helping one of my high school buddies take a whiz? If I were still
Jake's age, would I want to go to a movie if it meant holding a
straw to my friend's lips? If it meant the pee bottle?

———

Everywhere we went, people were unfailingly kind to Jake.
Waiters at restaurants, ushers at theatres, clerks at stores—
they would ask him (or me, as if under the impression that
Jake couldn't speak for himself) if he needed anything, anything at all. Despite their good intentions, their behaviour
sometimes seemed obsequious and inadvertently hurtful. At
the mall, some shoppers would take such a wide berth around
Jake's wheelchair that you'd think he had a disease that spread
through contact. I noticed how other people refused to make
eye contact, as if Jake travelled in a pocket of creeping shadows that inspired a rootless fear in them. And if *I* noticed, you
can bet Jake did, too. It pissed him off.

"It gives me the wheelchair angst," he'd say of this treatment.

Why did some people treat Jake that way? Those feelings
of pity or of gnawing fear—where did they come from? It
could have been nothing more than a sense of . . . *otherness*,
I guess, although that's not exactly the right or fair term.
Other only in the sense that the daily life of a person with
disabilities can differ drastically from that of a non-disabled
person—though of course, plenty of people with disabilities have lives similar to anyone's: responsibilities and jobs,

partners and children, often the same drudgery. But there are also those whose lives are much different. By that time I'd driven some kids who spent so much time at the Children's Hospital that they knew their doctors by first name and could compare notes on the best or worst hospital chow. Their days were a carousel of operations and recoveries, specialists, Wish Foundations, physiotherapy and counselling sessions. They took Prozac, Effexor, Zoloft, Adderall, or a cocktail of mood-alterers. Some, like Jake, got Botox injections in places I had never imagined Botox would go. Others had young bodies with old scars. Their lives followed a trajectory that you assumed held little in common with your own.

There was also the prospect of a person with profound special needs behaving in a manner you were unfamiliar or uncomfortable with. This wasn't the case with Jake, but he was an exception in some ways. Most of us follow basic rules of social decorum. But those hidebound rules aren't always a concern to individuals with special needs. It's not that they are unaware of them, just that they feel no urgency to abide by them. So within moments of meeting you that person might hug you or kiss your cheek or mouth or drop his trousers or pinch you or punch herself or refer to you as "mother" or "brother" or boldly state that you have a "horsey face." That person may moan or mutter or howl or laugh at nothing at all, or flap their arms like a bird or repeat the same question over and over or sing nonsense lyrics at a lung-rupturing pitch. That person may wear the brand of noise-baffling earmuffs people wear at shooting ranges, or lap at their hands compulsively in the manner of a cat, or offer impromptu karate demonstrations, winging wild kicks mere inches from your nose—I personally experienced every one of these interactions during my year as a bus driver. Any one of these encounters might leave a person feeling alarmed and confused, as well as sympathetic . . . which was how I often felt, even as my year on the road drew to a close. So, yes, I'll admit to the confusion and awkwardness and even the pity that I occasionally felt. But in the main, time and exposure made me understand that spending an afternoon with Jake was nothing to be worried about—so, even while I acknowledged the anxieties lurking behind those waiters' fawning platitudes and those shoppers who nearly flung themselves out of his wheelchair's path, it began to piss me off, too.

In high school, when I used to walk past the special needs class and glimpse those students in their sheltered world, my emotions had tangled into knots. Even now, having spent hundreds of hours with kids just like those students, they remain knotted. A few months earlier I'd driven a boy, Ethan, who snapped his body against his harness during the whole trip—the harnesses were a safety precaution but they looked like a straitjacket. Ethan hurled his body with such force that I could hear the compression of the leatherette upholstery, its horrible high-pitched squeal. And I let him do it. I had to. I'd been told it was useless to try to stop him, and I had realized by then that better minds than mine had surely tried.

Ethan had still been at that age where you could describe him as *beautiful*. A beautiful boy with long blond hair and soft, vaguely girlish features. Watching him snap himself against the restraints with unbridled venom, I thought: *What is going on inside that poor soul's head?* This had become one of my recurring thoughts: How do bodies get so broken? How do minds fail to control those bodies . . . and why are some of us so fortunate while others are not?

It's hard to accept percentages. That's what I found. No matter how small those percentages were, they still touched a lot of people—like the ripple of a stone tossed in a still pool, the one who is touched, like Ethan or Jake, touches so many other people: their fathers and mothers and grandparents and so on down the line. And there's no rhyme or reason as to how or why, is there? Which is why, when many of us encounter someone with a disability, our reflexive reaction is pity. We feel sorry for them, for how *unlucky* we sense they have been, and that sorrow is tinged with guilt at our own dumbshit luck.

—

Girls. Girls, girls, *girls*. Some days, girls were all Jake wanted to talk about. He was sixteen. It was his hormonal imperative.

"But nobody wants to date a guy who can't walk," he told me.

"I can walk and nobody wants to date me," I reminded him.

He said: "I want to date someone athletic."

"Like who, a powerlifter?"

"No. Shut up! Be serious. I want to be serious now."

"Why not a powerlifter?"

"I said shut up. Like, a girl who plays volleyball. But they all date football players."

I nodded sympathetically. "Some do. Not all of them."

"Too many of them."

"C'est la vie," I offered mock-philosophically, unwilling to indulge his maudlin ruminations.

"Do you have women troubles, Craig?"

I'd cancelled myself out of the dating game for a while by that time, judging myself unfit for human consumption. The last woman I'd dated ended our relationship by calling me emotionally unevolved. Had I misheard her? Had she said un*in*volved? But no, she was kind enough to repeat it: unevolved. The emotional equivalent of the Piltdown man. I'd idly considered printing up business cards to hand out to resigned-looking women.

Life Beaten You Down?

Willing to Try Just About Anything?

THINK:

Craig Davidson

555-555-5555

Jake was a handsome fellow. He had that flinty-cheek-boned English vibe going for him. Erudite, charming—*dashing*. Dark hair. Moody eyes. The ladies should have been falling all over him—and they would have been, if (a) he had been a touch more outgoing, and (b) he wasn't so self-conscious about the wheelchair. But the latter impacted the former. Sometimes I'd picture him beside the fire at a bush party, huddled under a blanket with a girl he fancied. Or in a car with one hand draped casually over the steering wheel and a girl riding shotgun. But no, those were old teenage fantasies of my own. I knew Jake's romantic entanglements, however they occurred, would be different—the particularities of his life demanded as much. Still, I sensed a deep longing from Jake that resonated with my own memories from that age. To want something so bad—a touch, a look—and to have no earthly clue how to get it, and then to see *someone else* get what you so dearly treasure . . . Love is tough at any age, but the bewilderment of love is never keener than when you're a teenager.

One day in mid-winter we were hanging out in the mall food court. I nodded to a girl about Jake's age in line at the A&W.

"You should go talk to her. Ask her to split a root beer float. Two straws."

Jake gave me a look. "Why don't you?" he said nervously.

"She's your age, man. Come on."

Jake turned it back on me. "You never talk to girls."

"Are you watching me every minute of every day?"

After much hemming and hawing, we worked out a deal. I agreed to talk to a random woman of Jake's selection. But Jake had to do the same thing. Jake knew I'd happily make a fool of myself for his amusement. And secretly, part of me was energized at the prospect of getting myself back in the game, half-assed as this attempt may have been.

Jake pointed at one woman. "How about her?"

"Jake, she's seventy years old."

"Okay, then. Her."

Now he was pointing at the seventy-year-old woman's companion, who was just as old.

"Is this a serious exercise or are you just screwing around?"

Jake stopped goofing off and put on his game face, scanning the food court for suitable candidates.

"How about that woman over there?"

He had singled out a gorgeous, glamorous woman waiting in line at Starbucks.

"Oh, please. Why not ask me to stick my face in a bear trap instead?"

"She is, like, a ten," Jake agreed. "You're . . . a four?"

"A *four*?" I was outraged. "So what you're saying is, I'm a fail. An attractiveness fail."

We settled on a woman roughly my age standing in line at the Dairy Queen. Why describe the encounter in detail? Suffice to say it was a regretful debacle, as forecasted from the start. I mumbled, "Butterfinger Blizzard, uh? Wise choice," like a bewildered and quite possibly senile sommelier. It went swiftly downhill from there. Within minutes I was slouching back to Jake.

"Rough?" he asked.

"Rough," I agreed.

"You suck at this."

"How *dare* you."

I had been convinced he'd beg off on his end of the bargain. But surprisingly, he was keen. It took nearly an hour for him to screw up his courage and settle on a girl he wanted to talk to. Cute, short black hair, holding a bag with a bookstore logo. Jake was a sucker for bookish girls. If she happened to play volleyball, so much the better.

As Jake began to manoeuvre through the throng towards her, the girl walked up a short flight of stairs to the food court's upper level. This meant Jake would have to flank around the stairs to the wheelchair ramp—and that might be just enough to deter him from going through with it. Jake saw fate lurking everywhere: if a pretty girl climbed up some stairs, thus making it slightly more difficult for him to talk to her, maybe that was fate's way of telling him to give up.

I was sure Jake would turn to me and say, "Forget it." But when he turned, it was with a determined expression on his face.

"A little help?"

No problem. I would have pancaked shoppers like an over-eager linebacker if he'd asked me to. We wended through the maze of people and up the wheelchair ramp; Jake found a seam in the traffic and shot the gap, the wheels of his chair making a zippering noise on the tiles. I held back, not wanting to intrude.

Jake must have said something because the girl turned, saw him, and smiled a little nervously. They began to talk. A minute went by. Two. Two and a half . . .

The girl *laughed*. She threw back her head and howled at something Jake had said. The sparkling sound of her laughter pealed off the high vaulted ceiling.

You sly dog, I thought.

When he came back, his face shone as brightly as a matchhead burst into flame. Fortune favours the brave, my son.

"Look at you," was all I could say.

Jake shrugged as if to say: *What did you expect? I'm irresistible. I'm catnip.*

Was I beholding a fresh monster—God help us all, a *player?*

"How did you do it, you devil? What did you talk about?"

Jake said, "A gentleman never tells."

———

Jake had good days and bad days, same as anyone. But his bad days could be really, *really* bad. Memories swarming his brain. Rage, sadness, frustration—and nowhere to put those feelings, no way to lessen the pressure. He'd sink into a funk and get down on his prospects. Things wouldn't work out the way they ought to, he was sure of it. They never had and never would.

It hurt me to see him like that. So I'd come up with a speech. I went so far as to write it down on a recipe card and put it in the bus's glovebox. Here's how it went:

Jake, as a teenager in high school you are presently in the most superficial environment known to mankind. Everything's about surface impressions. Everything's about how you look. How cool you are, whatever that means. If you've got a stylish hairdo and nice teeth and drive a Corvette . . . that's like, an entire person in high school. So if this isn't the time in your life when you excel with the ladies or where your true excellence is acknowledged, then hey, all I can say is: Welcome to the club. I suggest you work on those talents—your writing and intellect, your sense of humour and charm—that are going to have huge value down the line. Who wants to peak early, anyway? Play the long game. All the great stuff I see in you, which is so easily spotted by anybody with half a brain, is going to be appreciated in time. Just maybe not now, right this minute.

I sincerely planned to deliver that speech. And I never did. I guess I wasn't 100 percent sure I believed it myself. It put forward the notion that adulthood was a state of body and mind, or a point in time, where a person's worth was properly calibrated and surfaces ceased to matter. The cream would rise; adulthood would be the great equalizer. Perhaps that wouldn't have been a wholesale lie, but neither was it the truth as I saw it. I would have loved to tell Jake that high-school cool and adult cool were two different things. But I knew that the Brad Pitts of this world had been cool in high school, too. Guys like that were born with the coolness gene hardwired into their DNA. I would have loved to tell Jake that bullying stops when you're an adult. But one of the most painful understandings I'd reached was that it doesn't. A lot of people grow older but never grow *up*. Bullies still existed in adulthood—they just found subtler means to ply their trade, and sadly, those methods often worked. And did the square-jawed QB *not* marry the leggy volleyball player? Of course they did. They married each other much more often than the QB romanced the band spaz, or the winsome volleyball player hooked up with the AV club dweeb. Things change in adulthood, sure. But they stayed the same in a lot of important ways, too.

What chewed me up was the fact that Jake's struggle made sense. Jake's passions were different from those of other kids his age because of the different kind of life he'd lived. The fact that he preferred fantasy to reality made sense. The fact that other teenagers had difficulty relating to Jake made sense, too. And so, given that all these things made sense, it followed that Jake might indeed spend much of his life struggling against isolation. The way I saw it, the ones and twos added up with a perfect, terrifying logic.

"If his schoolmates hung out with Jake more often," Calvin would say to me, "they would see the handicap is no big deal. Plus they'll feel good about themselves."

I agreed with him, but I also understood why something that seemed so simple was so hard.

The only other serious topic Jake and I dipped into was that of Jake's mother. I got the impression a lot of people were pushing Jake to open up about the accident. I also got the impression Jake didn't want me to be one of those people. So we didn't talk about it much.

"If Mom hadn't died," he did say one day, "so many things wouldn't have happened. We wouldn't have gone to Disneyland for Christmas—Mom would never have accepted the Make-A-Wish Foundation's offer. I wouldn't have learned to cook a casserole because Mom said it was too much of a hassle to let me cook. I would never have met you."

"We probably would have met, Jake. I'd still have driven your bus."

He nodded. "Okay, probably."

"But fate. I get it."

"That's what I mean. You meet people and your life gets its shape by the things that happen when you meet."

——

By and large, and despite the challenges, the days Jake and I shared that year were joyful. And by thunder, we had fun: hours and hours of laughing our fool asses off. We developed our own dialect hewn out of scraps of pop culture ephemera and characters spawned by our own crazed imaginations. Which was how I knew I'd made a true friend: we spoke our own language.

"Let's play 'Wave Upon Wave,' Craig."

"Sounds good. You start."

"I'll send wave upon wave of Chinese Hunting Bees upon you!"

"Then I'll send wave upon wave of angry mall Santas upon you!"

"Then I'll send wave upon wave of cinnamon-coated Carpet Bandits!"

"What?" Laughing so hard I couldn't hear properly. "Carpet-baggers?"

"Carpet *Bandits!*"

"I'll send wave upon wave of illiterate anchormen armed with pocket knives!"

"I'll send wave upon wave of synthesizing robots!"

"That doesn't sound too bad, Jake."

"Yeah, but they're maniacal!"

"Whaaa!"

"Whaaaaaah!"

On and on it would go, until we were both braying like donkeys and Jake began to make his alarming choking sounds.

"You must stop! I can't *breathe.*"

The only earnest thing I ever made a point of repeating—and I said this to Jake on a regular basis—was that he was the toughest son of a gun I'd ever met.

"Anybody who's been hit by a truck, been in a coma, and still resides under blue sky can't be anything but a total badass."

"Badass?" Jake would make a face. "I still like *Thomas the Tank Engine.*"

"Well," I reasoned, "who says trains aren't totally badass?"

And Jake *was* tough. Not just physically. Anyone who had endured such immense loss and grief and uncertainty had to be almost superhumanly tough in an emotional and spiritual sense.

"I'm so happy today," he would often say, "and I have no idea *why*."

One day as that apocalyptic winter was finally ceding, when patches of browned grass could be glimpsed through the snow crust, it was just me and Jake in the bus, rolling slowly towards his house, savouring the taste of spring in the air.

Out of nowhere, Jake said: "Dad and I think of you as my big brother, Craig."

I was stunned into silence for a moment. What should I say to that? It seemed an enormous responsibility. And with a pang I realized I wasn't sure I was a great big brother to the sibling I already had.

"Oh. Thanks, dude."

"Okay. Just wanted to say it."

And we left it at that.

SPRING

From
"THE SEEKERS,"
an unpublished novel

Ripley eyed the spider on the wall above her bed. A tiny silver spider like a bead of mercury with legs.

The room was bigger than her punishment cell at the Grand Isle School. Bed, sink, toilet. Spotless white walls and floor. So white it hurt her eyes.

She had been taken to the room shortly after entering the compound. The boys were taken somewhere else. Ripley had wanted to run—a voice in her head was screaming, *Get out of here, now!*—but the driver had a pistol and the fence was topped with razor-wire that would have sliced her to ribbons, and past that lay the woods: dark, deep, endless.

Someone had left a pair of navy overalls on the bed. Ripley changed into them and sat cross-legged on the mattress. The spider crawled from a tiny hole where two walls met the ceiling. It was good to know that even in a place like this, nature could find a way in. In a million years when this building was dust, the spiders would still be here.

The door opened. The man she had met back at Grand Isle stepped inside.

"Hello again," he said. "My name is Christopher. Sorry for the late introduction."

Ripley couldn't recall another time when an adult had introduced himself to her by his first name.

"I am going to be your guide through all this, Ms. Ripley. Please, come with me."

"Where are we going?"

"We're already here, Ms. Ripley."

"Who are you, the Cheshire Cat? What is all this?"

"Every adventure requires a first step," said Christopher, marching out of the room.

After a moment's hesitation, she followed him down an antiseptically white hallway. The floor declined gradually under her feet. She could hear the steady hum of machinery behind the walls.

At last they came to a door with a wheel on its outside, like the ones you see on bank vaults. Christopher punched numbers on a keypad. The hiss of compressed air. He cranked the wheel and threw his weight against the door to push it open.

"Don't be afraid," he said. "You're supposed to be here, Ms. Ripley. This is where you belong."

A shiver travelled down Ripley's spine. She had no earthly idea where she belonged, so how could this guy?

She stepped through the door. Her breath caught.

"Welcome home," she heard Christopher say.

The room's walls went up and up to meet a ceiling that must have been two hundred yards above the floor. Everything was the same dazzling white as her room. She couldn't see any lights—so where was it coming from? From all around it seemed as if the walls had been built of pure light. The floor was bare whitewashed cement. Four folding metal chairs sat in the centre of the immense room.

Christopher shut the door behind them. Its outline disappeared: the wall looked whole, as if they had stepped right through it. He led her to the chairs and offered her one. She sat.

A square of darkness appeared in the far wall. Another door opening, she realized. The big boy stepped through it. Christopher called out: "Over here, Gavin!"

The large boy—Gavin, apparently—walked over. It took him a while: the room was that big, and Gavin's head swivelled to take it all in. He wore the same overalls as she did. He glanced at Ripley—the skin crinkled at the edges of his eyes, but his lips didn't smile—then sat down.

Another door opened to their left. Oliver stepped through. His voice drifted up to the ceiling. "Whoa."

He sauntered over, clearly trying not to look overwhelmed. He kept making a gesture as if to slip his hands into the pockets of his overalls—but they didn't have pockets, so his hands slid uselessly down his thighs with a whispery sound.

Once Oliver was seated, Christopher pulled the fourth chair around and sat facing them.

"I imagine you have some questions," he said.

"Give the man a cigar," said Oliver.

Ripley had so many questions that they nearly overloaded her brain.

Why are we here?

Who are you?

Who are these other two?

What did we do?

Are you going to let us go?

"Why us?" was the question she settled on.

Christopher knit his hands on his lap. "The answer to that—like a lot of things I'm going to tell you—will sound crazy."

"As crazy as a freakin' pyramid in the middle of the woods?" said Oliver. "The bar's set pretty high."

"I'm glad you see it that way, Mr. Cooke," Christopher said. "Now, Ms. Ripley, as for your question: the simplest but most confusing answer would be that you're here now because you've been here before. You're coming back."

Now *that* was crazy. Ripley had never set eyes on this place. She would have remembered. And she would have run as fast as she could in the opposite direction.

"Your names were on a list." Christopher spread his hands. "A list that came from . . . well, from the future."

"I get it," Oliver said, eyeing Christopher cagily. "You're

some rich weirdo, right? Did you build this place? Is this
some kind of game? Okay, I'll play along. Whatever you
want. We can climb into your cardboard time machine and
go look at dinosaurs together."

Another square of darkness appeared in the wall. A third
boy came through it. He was in a wheelchair. The boy rolled
his chair over to them slowly; Ripley could feel him sizing
everyone up. He was slender, with dark hair that fell over
one of his eyes. He wore the kind of fingerless gloves that
weightlifters used.

Christopher said, "Jake, meet Ms. Ripley, Mr. Cooke, and
Mr. Leon."

The boy nodded at them—a sharp, not entirely friendly
gesture.

"Nice of you to bring your own chair," Oliver said to Jake.

"Nice of you to use so little of your own," Jake shot back.

Oliver's head rocked back as if he'd been punched.
He rubbed his jaw and stared at Jake with a newfound
appreciation.

"Ms. Ripley just asked me why the four of you are here,"
Christopher said to Jake.

"The five of us," Jake said.

"Yes, we'll get to him," Christopher went on. "I told them
about the list. Mr. Cooke seems to think this is some elaborate joke."

"I wish it was," said Jake.

Christopher said, "But it's not, is it?"

Jake turned his gaze on Ripley and the other two.

"No," he said. "It's not."

"So as to why you're here—I mean, you four specifically," said Christopher. "I can't tell you that. Maybe you volunteered. Or maybe you were selected based on your natural capabilities. Whatever the case, you ended up on the list."

"I don't have any capabilities," said Ripley.

Christopher said, "You have no idea what you're capable of, Ms. Ripley. We will train you. Here, over the coming months."

"Train us for what?" Oliver said.

Christopher and Jake exchanged a glance. They both looked weary.

"You will not believe what I'm going to tell you now, either," said Christopher. "But you will in time."

"Oh, I'm all ears," Oliver said scathingly.

"This place—everything you see—was not built in the past. It was built in the future," Christopher said. "It simply appeared. One day—one *second*—it did not exist. The next, it did. And this building holds the answers as to why it appeared. There is no place like it on earth. The potential power within these walls is incalculable. So we must be very, very careful."

Nobody said anything. Not even Oliver.

14.

The term *special needs* encompasses a vast spectrum of physical, cognitive, and emotional conditions. Most of the kids on my regular bus sat on the mild end of that spectrum. But when I took on routes as a substitute driver I encountered kids on the acute end. Kids who spoke not a word, who laughed endlessly, or who bucked riotously in their restraints. I drove kids who appeared to exist in a world of their own summoning, locked inside their heads with no door to the outside. I drove kids who were the equivalent of nitroglycerine—handle them with reverence or else, *ka-boom*.

When I was substitute-driving I came away from some encounters with the impression that these kids actually *felt* things differently, not simply that they ignored or failed to interpret social cues. Maybe I was wrong—there's a more-than-reasonable chance that I was simply ignorant. Still, from my vantage, I got the sense that these kids felt emotions that were on a different register of intensity than those felt by many of us. I found it impossible to get a read on these children: it was like trying to dig my fingers into porcelain. They laughed or cried for reasons seemingly unrelated to their present circumstances. They might look at a rainbow and cry. Or stare at roadkill and laugh. Unable to modulate their emotions, they sprayed laughter and tears like an unattended fire hose . . . or again, perhaps I was failing to see the nuances of their emotional or mental states.

I remember one boy on a substitute route, Benson. Fifteen years old. He wore a parka no matter the season. He also wore giant noise-baffling ear protectors, the kind you see at gun ranges. One day, I caught him crying in his seat. Alarmed, I pulled over.

"What's the matter, Benson?"

He stared at me, apparently cleansed of comprehension.

"He cries all the time," his classmate told me. "He just cries and cries."

Benson would also repeat phrases in a high, excited, urbane voice. "I'm having a lovely time" and "I'm very happy to be here" and "Benson, come oooon down!"—the way Rod Roddy used to say it on *The Price Is Right*. Sometimes these phrases seemed tangentially connected to whatever was going on. For example, when a dark cloud passed over the sun, he'd say: "It was a dark and stooormy night." Or when I braked hard for a yellow light: "I'm getting N-E-R-V-O-U-S. Don't be silly, Arthur, you're going to be just fine."

It took me a while to realize that every word Benson spoke was cribbed from television shows. When I glanced at him in the riot mirror I was often struck by just how handsome this boy was. Ethan, the boy who fought against his restraints, was handsome in the same way: their faces unlined, their eyes a piercing blue and their hair a wispy blond. They both had that bracing movie-star handsomeness. I pictured Benson on a park bench. A cute girl sits beside him. She tries to engage him in conversation ("I'm having a lovely time") before the realization dawns on her, too: this heartbreakingly beautiful boy has a personality inaccessible not only to her, but to almost everyone.

Ungrippable. That was the word that leapt to my mind when I thought about the Bensons and Ethans I drove. Benson's needs and desires and fears . . . I couldn't gain access to them. I don't know that *anybody* could. It must've been rough for a parent, I thought, to never really know how their child was feeling—no fine shadings, anyway, nothing more than a broad happy or sad. And therein, I realized, must lie both fear and hope: fear that there was nothing more . . . and hope that there *was*, but (and with this came fear again) it was impossible for Benson to share that part of himself with anyone.

Kids, I was beginning to understand, are finely calibrated instruments. They break in subtle ways, often difficult to intuit. The good news? They often repair themselves quickly, forgetting those past hurts. The bad news: sometimes the break is deep, and it is hard to find the remedy.

During training, all of us drivers learned the "Special Needs Cycle." If a child is exhibiting signal behaviours—chewing their clothes, yelping, crying, laughing forcefully at nothing—it may be wise to intervene in hopes of stemming an outburst. Frequently, though, nothing will help. In that case, you brace for a meltdown.

Meltdown was the most widely used term for an outburst. Even the kids on the bus used it off-handedly.

"Sorry," Oliver might say if he and Gavin were late to the bus after school. "Some kid had a meltdown in class."

"I forgot to take my meds," Oliver casually informed me on another occasion, "and had a meltdown at the zoo. Mom had a total panic attack."

During that year I faced a child flinging his body around hard enough to split himself in half, screaming, crying, punching the seat and laughing all at once. Other meltdowns were deeply internal: a child tensed into a ball, weeping on and on. I discovered I preferred the overt ones; the soft ongoing weeping kicked so much harder at your heart. I also learned that meltdowns can be contagious. One kid melts down and it spreads to another kid, then another, until you've got a busload of meltdowns all happening at once. What's worse, the kids not having meltdowns begin to berate the kids having them:

"Shut up!" they'll scream. "Get it together, you weirdo!"

Meltdowns can happen without warning. A switch wired to every impulse centre inside a child's head gets flipped. For a few minutes you're dealing with the equivalent of a

Tasmanian devil. When a child has a meltdown, it's no use haranguing or threatening. You assess the direness. Is the child biting or clawing at himself? Is he a danger to anyone else? If not, what I always did was gently grasp the child's shoulder. I would feel this organic electricity pulsing up my arm as it poured out of the child. That simple human contact can go a long way. It doesn't stop a meltdown but it can drop it several degrees, like Advil counteracting a fever.

One time Benson had a meltdown. He screamed and cried and hammered his skull off the window. It terrified me, as that level of self-harm always did. I pulled the bus over and hustled down the aisle and placed my hand on his shoulder. He stopped hitting his head. He held one hand up to me with his fingers outspread. Weeping, twisting, moaning. I laid my palm flat on his, spreading my fingers to touch the tips to Benson's, same as you do when comparing hand size with someone. Benson slipped his fingers between mine and squeezed. Simple human contact. Blood-warmed flesh on flesh. In that one instance—that *one time*—it worked. It wasn't always so easy.

Gavin had only one meltdown all year—although I'm not even sure you could call it that. As meltdowns went, it was almost Zen-like. The high school had a PD day when it happened. Oliver was off sick. As a result, Gavin was my only rider, and when I pulled up to his stop to collect him, he was crying. Not bawling, not a mess—it was the stifled, stiff-upper-lip variety of weeping.

"I don't know what's the matter," his home care aide told me worriedly. "Some kind of disruption to his schedule this morning, is what his mother told me."

Gavin's life was dominated by routines. When he stepped off the bus at his school, he would circle the trashcan near the school doors three times. In the winter, a snowy hillock encircled the can; he'd circle it doggedly, slipping a bit. Gavin may not have been totally aware of the passage of time, may not have paid attention to the movements of hands on a clock, but his days were nonetheless carefully ordered. Every morning he circled that trashcan. Every day he sat on his same seat in the bus. Every day we'd play the seat belt game, where he slyly unclicked his belt and I'd follow up with a faux-wrathful, "Gaaa-VIN!" Every day we'd merge onto the highway and he'd say: "Whoa!" Every day the same. It was how Gavin liked it—his world orderly and sensible.

When those little routines got upset, well, Gavin got upset. So that morning when Gavin was crying, it distressed me. I'd never seen Gavin visibly angry. Never seen him overtly sad. This had fostered in me the misguided belief that his emotional repertoire lacked these notes; he'd seemed such a preternaturally well-adjusted boy that his obvious sorrow threw me into a tizzy.

That morning he got on the bus in misery, but he didn't cause a fuss. He wept silently, shoulders hitching. He wore a toque despite the warmness of the day, pulling it over his eyes. Snuffling, his chin trembling. He lifted his toque and gazed out the window. A great big sigh. I caught his eyes in the riot mirror. He brought one hand—such big hands, a carpenter's hands—up to shield his face.

"It's all right, Gav," I said. "You do whatever you need to do. If you need to cry, it's just fine by me. We all need to cry sometimes."

We veered onto the 22X highway skirting the city's southern edge. "Whoa!" said Gavin, as always. Next he was crying again. It gutted me. But nobody can be expected to have a sunny disposition all the time, I reminded myself. I had no clue why he was upset or what had triggered his weeping, and since Gavin couldn't articulate his distress to me in any way that I could have grasped, it was all but impossible to help.

"Buck up, big guy," I said companionably. "Or else I'm bound to start with the waterworks, too. The two of us tooling down the road crying our guts out."

By the time I picked him up that afternoon, he was good as gold.

——

Oliver was the one ever-present meltdown risk. Initially I thought his volatility was sugar-related. Oliver had such hairtrigger tolerance that he could eat a tangerine and go batshit. I put the bus on sugar lockdown. Nobody was allowed to share their sweets with Oliver. Harsh and dictatorial? Sure, but the bus would have been a madhouse otherwise.

These measures didn't stop the meltdowns, however. While sugar was clearly an accelerant, I now believe the real problem was hyperarousal—a common concern with Fragile X kids. The world's stimuli came on with such intensity that it simply swamped Oliver.

Sometimes I was able to intervene and head off the meltdown. One spring afternoon Oliver was sprinting from the schoolyard to the bus. His sneaker got sucked into the mud and was pulled off his foot. He ran a few steps sneakerless before hopping back to retrieve it. At first he was laughing.

"Did you see that?" he said. "It's because I'm such a fast sprinter."

But as Oliver assessed the damage, he became more and more agitated. There was mud on his shoe, and his sock. Worst of all, there was mud on his sister's skinny jeans—which he wore because he thought he looked especially good in skinny jeans.

"Oh, schizz!" he howled. "My jeans. Hell-hell-hell!"

I was navigating through the school zone. Kids were zipping around me on bikes and skateboards. Preoccupied with this, I missed the signs of the looming meltdown.

That's when Oliver screamed: "*Fuuuuck!*"

"Whoa!" went Gavin.

I pulled over. "Oliver, buddy, what's the deal?"

"My jeans are all muddy! Mom's going to kill me!"

By then he was crying. Great wracking sobs. Oliver's pale face was swollen round the tear ducts; his eyes were so much bluer when encircled by the inflamed red of his sockets.

My bus was a touchy-feely zone. There was a regular caval-
cade of fist-bumping, high-fiving, and back-patting. I culti-
vated a physical informality between me and every one of the
kids—I never pushed it, but the kids were okay with it. So
when I parked the bus and walked down the aisle and gently
touched Oliver's shoulder, he only shuddered briefly before
calming down.

"Okay," I said. "Let's think. You want to hear my plan?"

Oliver sniffled, then—somewhat grudgingly, and for-
lornly—he nodded.

"Here's what you're going to do. I'll drop you off early. I'll
change the route today, okay? I'll take you home first. Is your
mom going to be home?"

Oliver shook his head.

"Perfect. You've got another pair of jeans, right?"

Oliver paused, then nodded again.

"Great. Now you go home and take off these jeans. And
the socks. Do you know how to use your washing machine?"

"No."

"That's okay. What you do is, stuff the jeans and socks
down the bottom of your hamper. Cover them with dirty
clothes. Put on another pair of jeans."

Oliver said: "Or shorts?"

"Shorts, sure. Put your sneakers out on the deck. Once
the mud dries, smack the soles together. That mud will just
fly off. Or you could clean them with the hose, if you're careful. Okay?"

Oliver sniffed, smiling now. "Okay."

"What your mom doesn't know won't kill her, right?"

"Right."

I headed back to the wheel feeling like Winston Wolfe, Harvey Keitel's "cleaner" character in *Pulp Fiction*.

Are you a thirteen-year-old with a minor domestic problem? Muddy duds? Dry those eyes. Call The Bus Driver. He's got your back.

Other times I wasn't so lucky. There were always harbingers with Oliver, yes, but often by the time I took note of them it was like trying to disarm dynamite once the fuse had burnt down into the stick. At that point you could only wait for the *BOOM*.

It usually started with Oliver's pre-meltdown laugh: a staccato *Ha!Ha!Ha!*, more a belch than a laugh. Then he'd segue into his "Mad Scientist" persona: affecting a high-pitched, nasal twang, he would start to issue threatening pronouncements.

"I'm going to get a twelve-gauge shotgun and blow the *schiizzz* out of this bus!"

Ha!Ha!Ha!

"I'm going to fill a needle with poison and inject it into your *braaaains!*"

Ha!Ha!Ha!

If I were near Oliver's home when the Mad Scientist reared his ugly bulbous head, I'd just drop him off. Go with God, son. I figured the open air would drop his arousal levels.

On other occasions, I'd have to pull over.

"First of all, Oliver, you can't threaten anyone on this bus," I'd tell him. "Joke or no joke. Everyone has to treat everyone else with respect. I'm not moving until you've settled down. So everyone will have to wait."

The other kids would then pile on Oliver, complaining he was keeping them from going home. Sometimes it worked. But on one or two occasions this led to simultaneous melt-downs: a few kids would get mad at Oliver, Oliver would start screaming, then Vincent or Nadja might start screaming *back*, and the situation devolved. A lot of my kids were medicated. As I recall, Vincent took Prozac. Gavin took Prozac or Xanax. I think Oliver was on Ritalin and some other stuff. Jake was on a cocktail of this and that. So when a meltdown occurred, I wondered how much of it was a factor of the meds they were on, how much of it was their condition presenting itself, and how much was just a case of a kid being a kid?

At the beginning of the year, I had made the mistake of assuming these kids were saints. I'd nursed a short-lived belief that they embodied all the best traits of humanity and none of the bad. So when they had the same lapses in compassion as anyone else, my foolish heart shattered a little. And believe me, I soon witnessed instances of true awfulness. There were times I got so angry it took every drop of willpower not to pull over and punt the offending student onto the street.

An example: There was a running joke on our bus about leaving somebody behind in the woods. If one of the kids started to bellyache about their drop-off order, I'd say: "It's your lucky day, then. Your parents told me to drop you off in the woods."

This was met with the standard reply: "Yeah, *right*."

One afternoon I had to drop Jake off first; he had to be home early to get to physiotherapy. This marked a change in the routine. Oliver was forced to sit on the bus longer than normal. He began to transform into the Mad Scientist.

Jake's house was always last on the route, so none of the other kids had ever seen it. Jake decided to joke about this, invoking our old standby about leaving people in the woods.

"My house is already in the woods," Jake said, "so I don't have to find my way home."

"Actually," I said, continuing the joke, "I drop Jake off at an elevator that takes him up to his house on a cloud."

"My mom lives on a cloud," Jake said quietly.

I instantly regretted my remark. At around this time, Oliver hit hyperarousal. He laughed hysterically, in jagged coughing bursts. The Mad Scientist was *alive*.

"Why's your mom on a cloud?" he asked.

Jake had never spoken about his mother to anyone.

"She died," Jake said.

"Died? Your mom's *dead*?"

Jake concentrated on the floor. "Yes."

Oliver laughed. The little shit *laughed*.

Ha! Ha! Ha!

He drew his thumb across his neck in a throat-slitting gesture. "You mean she's *shriiiik*—like, dead?"

"Hey!" I said, deeply pissed. "That's not how you talk about
stuff like that."

"What did I do?" said Oliver. "She's dead, right? He said so,
so I said it."

"You can't just say anything you like," I said. "Not if it's
nasty."

"Well, you're just going to have to get used to it."

My eyes darted to the riot mirror. Oliver stared back
challengingly. He truly believed he'd offered no more than
a statement of fact—which in truth was all he *had* done.
Still, hurtful truths had no place on my bus. I realized then
that I wasn't dealing with Oliver but rather the hyperaroused
variation, the Mad Scientist, who I'd allowed out of his box
through my inattention.

"You're not showing any respect, Oliver. Show some."

"Make me."

My grip tightened on the wheel. He was a kid. I *liked* Oliver.
But if buses had come with ejector buttons I'd have grinningly
catapulted him into the stratosphere.

"I *will* make you, Oliver. That was your first and last
warning."

Something in the tone of my voice was enough to make the
Mad Scientist get the hell out of Dodge. "I was only joking,"
Oliver said meekly.

We pulled up at Jake's house. Oliver continued to wax apologetic.

"I'm sorry," he said to Jake. "You must miss your mom a lot, right?"

"It's all right," Jake said. "Yes. I miss her."

I got out and lowered the ramp for Jake. I felt massive guilt for letting Oliver spiral into a state where he could be expected to make uncomplicatedly cruel statements.

"When Oliver gets that way," I told Jake, ". . . you know."

"I know. It's okay, Craig."

What else could Jake do? He couldn't even face his antagonist: his wheelchair sat in a fixed position, facing the front. He could only accept Oliver's words and assume they were the product of ignorance. I wish he could've slugged Oliver, just to make things fair. I wouldn't have allowed it, of course, but I dearly wished Jake had that outlet. Yet my wishing for powers beyond his grasp was a wish for him to be somebody else entirely. Jake's limitations were part of what made him who he was. Same went for Oliver. And, I realized as I watched Jake pilot his wheelchair up the drive, the same went for me—and everyone else on this spinning lump of rock and ice we all call home.

15.

Best day on the job?

I awoke in honeyed sunlight. Pulled on socks, jeans, wool sweater. I called it in.

"Craig Davidson, route 412."

Set off across the soccer field towards the school parking lot. The earth held that ozone smell it had after a rainstorm, a rich mineral tang you can taste at the back of your throat. Dark clouds braided the horizon to the west, the recent downpour having moved on.

The bus looked fine. Suspiciously so. Nothing busted or spraypainted. But after unlocking the door and stepping inside, I was assaulted by the astringent stink of gunpowder. The driver's seat was covered in bits of brightly coloured paper. A scorchmark was burnt on the rubberized flooring of the entry stairs.

Vandals! *Again!* I pieced their outrageous attack together. They must have jammed firecrackers between the rubberized lips of the bus doors, figuring they could blow them open the way safe crackers blew bank vaults apart in the movies. The jumped-up, rat-assed little twerps! I swept the tatters of charred paper up. No real damage done, aside from the lingering smell.

Would I be spending *another* night in the bus? No. Be an adult, Davidson, for once in your life!

I finished my pre-route inspection and pulled onto the road. When I arrived at Jake's house, the garage door was still closed. When it finally rattled up, Jake and his father exited silently. Calvin finished his cigarette while I strapped Jake's chair down. Jake offered only a terse, "Good morning, Craig."

When we were ready to go, Calvin hopped on board.

"Now, I want to ask you something," he said to his son.

"Dad . . ."

"No, no," Calvin said, "I'm going to ask you in front of Craig."

Calvin hunched down and looked Jake straight in the eye.

"Those things you said to me. Cruel things. Would you have said them to Craig?"

Jake didn't answer.

"You wouldn't have, no," Calvin went on. "Right. And why? Because the two of you are friends, yeah?"

Jake's gaze was determinedly fixed on something out the window.

"I'll tell you what my own mother used to say when I was being a little shit," Calvin said. "Sometimes I wish you'd treat me like a stranger, my son."

A span of silence. Calvin softened.

"It's rough right now," he said, outlining the family's situation with bracing plainness. "You lost your mother. I lost my wife. But Jake, we can't . . . *wallow.*"

"I know, Dad. I'm sorry."

"You don't have to be sorry. What's there to be sorry about?"

Calvin gripped the back of Jake's head and pressed their foreheads together.

"I love you."

"I know."

"We should say it every day."

"Dad . . ."

Calvin relented. "Have a good day. Head up, so the girls can see your eyes."

"Dad."

"*Positive.* Stay positive."

We pulled onto the road. For the first few minutes Jake didn't speak. No use pushing it. Once we were a few miles from home he opened up. We yakked about the usual glib stuff—a hot topic was the pretty girl in social studies class he was desperately trying to strike up a conversation with.

"Soooooo," Jake said, trying out a line, "do you like . . . stuff?"

"Soooooo," I parried, "want to come over and look at my etchings?"

Jake's brow furrowed. "Etchings?"

Sometimes I forgot the age gap between the two of us. Some of the things I said sailed over his head, and vice-versa.

"It's a cheesy old pickup line," I said. "Same as, *You want to go watch the submarine races?*"

"I don't get it."

"It was code for, like, 'Want to park the car beside the river and make out?'"

"Why? Still don't get it."

"Because you can't watch a submarine race, right? It's underwater."

"*Still* don't get it."

I let it go. The boy was being purposefully obtuse, which usually meant he wanted to switch the subject. He told me about a dream he'd had.

"We were on a train. We were late for a play. I had the lead role. Dad was there, and Molly, and Mom and you, too. We missed the play because the train hurtled right past the theatre. It went all the way down to Mexico and stopped at a gas station. Then a Mexican witch doctor turned Molly into a bottle of tequila."

I laughed. "That's so random."

"Yes, but then that dream ended and a different one started. In the new dream I was a butterfly. A tiny butterfly and all white. Sort of like that condition where you can't be out in the sun . . ."

"Albino."

"An albino butterfly. I must have been laid late as an egg or stuck in my cocoon because by the time I'm born it's nearly winter. I'm flying and snowflakes are falling and when one of them hits my wing it's like being hit with a heavy pillow. And I'm scared but I don't really know I'm scared because I'm a butterfly and butterflies don't feel fear. Then next, I'm not looking out of my butterfly eyes anymore. I'm watching from a little distance away through someone else's eyes I guess, maybe God's eyes. I'm watching myself in the snowstorm and it's falling very steady now, very hard, it's getting dark and I can't make myself out anymore in the snow and I know I'll die soon. But I've only just been born."

"Heavy stuff," was all I could say. "Well, what do you think?"

"About what?"

"You think it means anything?"

Jake frowned. "Smoke me a kipper, I'll be home for breakfast!"

This was a line from Jake's favourite sitcom at that time, *Red Dwarf*. It was also a cue to drop the subject. Back to silliness.

We pulled up in front of Vincent's house. He waited in his driveway, hitching up his pants.

"Top o' the morning, Vincent old chum," I said.

"Heeeeey . . . ask me about *Staaar Waaars*. I know eeeeverything."

I swung around a cul-de-sac and backtracked to pick up Oliver, who was waiting under a honeysuckle tree wearing an oversized black hoodie, resembling a slender version of Friar Tuck.

"Hey guys," he said as he clambered aboard, "guess what?"

"Whaaaaat?"

Fifteen seconds elapsed. Oliver was already seated and belted in before he spoke.

"Did you know that if you fly a fighter jet at a hundred miles per hour over the city, that the police will come and arrest you?" When nobody reacted to this, Oliver said: "When I was two years old, my brain weighed ten pounds."

I navigated out of Vincent and Oliver's suburban neighbourhood and crossed a major intersection to arrive at Nadja's condo complex.

"Good morning, Craig. How are you?"

"Peachy keen, Nadja."

"I'm nice, too. It's a very nice day. Do you want to know what I did last night?"

"Okay. Shoot."

"I went to my auntie's house for a dinner party."

"Uh-huh."

"And by the way, my auntie has a sister in India? And she got stomach trouble one day and the trouble got worse? And by the way, she died."

"That's awful, Nadja. Truly heartbreaking."

I arrived at my first school and dropped off Jake, Nadja, and Vincent. While lowering the ramp for Jake, I said:

"Today, my friend. Talk to that girl in social studies."

"We'll see," Jake said.

"At least keep your head up so she can see your eyes."

"Craig . . ." Jake growled threateningly.

I got back on the road, heading towards Gavin's house.

Oliver asked, "What are you doing this weekend?"

"No plans," I said. "What about you?"

"Fixing my dirtbike. Oil change, spark plugs. You know."

I said, "Cool. Can I get a look at your bike when I drop you off tonight?"

"You could, except my dad sold it," Oliver said warily.

"Is that so? When did he sell it?"

"Now. Just this minute."

"Bummer."

"Yeah. I loved that bike."

We idled at Gavin's stop while he donned his shoes and sweater. That fleeting instant of eye contact passed between us. Once he was belted in, we rolled. The CB radio crackled.

"Base to unit 2312."

"2312 by."

"Be advised that the pickup time for your kindergarten route has changed from 11:40 to 12:10. The students have a nap they must attend."

I glanced in the riot mirror. Oliver was making cartoonish punching sounds—*Pffbt! Pffbt!*—as he swung his fists. Alarmed, worried that he might be boiling towards a meltdown, I asked what he was doing.

"Oh, y'know," he said matter-of-factly. "Just beating up this monster that was bugging Gavin."

Gavin peeked around his seat at the ground where the invisible monster apparently lay, bloodied and beaten following Oliver's assault.

"A monster, huh? Any specific type, or just your run-of-the-mill?" I asked.

A few more punching noises: *Crack! Baff!*

"Yeah, a regular monster," said Oliver in that breezy way of his. "That's about the siiiiize of it."

Thank goodness our bus had a resident monster slayer. Gavin gazed at Oliver with an expression of relief. Oliver said: "If he gives you any more trouble, Gavvy, let me know."

When we pulled up at the school, I said, "All right, soldiers. Out of the bus and into the breech."

Oliver drew his hood up over his blond locks and sallied forth. But Gavin wasn't budging. I scrolled through my mental jukebox. A little ditty by Jim Croce should do the trick.

Now the south side of Cowtown
That's a bad place, not a haven
And if you you're gonna go there, son you best beware
Of a dude named Bad ole Gavin;
Yeah, he's mad, bad Gavvy Gav
Meanest lad in the whole damn pad
Badder than old King Kow-wooong
Meaner than a junkyard dawg!

Gavin was out the door like he'd been fired from a circus cannon. He circled the trashcan three times, gave me a hesitant wave and headed into school.

Huge wet snowflakes tumbled from the sky as I drove

home. I parked and walked down the street. When I exited my house five hours later the snow had already melted. The air was brilliant, raw, the smell of new life pushing through the earth. The streets were slick and shiny with melt.

I drove to the middle school through a storm of cottonwood dander. When the bell rang, the student body poured out into the strong sunshine. Oliver darted through the milling crowd, moving nimbly, surfing the tide of student bodies. Gavin wasn't far behind.

Man, I loved watching Gavin run to the bus. Head down like a bull charging at a toreador's red cape. As he was chugging along that afternoon, his trousers sagged a little lower and a little lower until—

"Gavin's pants fell off!" Oliver cried.

It wasn't a total de-pantsing. Gavin's trousers snagged just above the knees. Thankfully, his underwear was in good shape. No holes. He shrugged off his backpack and yanked his trousers up. Then he was on his horse again.

"That was some kind of wardrobe malfunction," I said as he clambered aboard. Gavin wasn't the least bit sheepish. Could it be that he'd liked being the centre of attention for once?

"Your pants fell down!" Oliver was still reeling. "Craig, Gavin's *pants* fell *down!*"

Ten minutes later I pulled into the high school. Teenagers in ragtops and old beaters navigated the parking lot. My kids bombed into the bus. Much grousing and switching of seat partners ensued. I headed out to lower the ramp for Jake.

"I couldn't do it," he moaned. "I couldn't talk to her."

"Oh, dude."

"She was right there, Craig. Standing in front of me. Gaaah!"

"Buck up, chum. There's still time left in the year."

"She was so close," he said theatrically. "*Aaaargh!*"

It was tight quarters inside the bus. I manoeuvred through a warren of backpacks and legs and knelt behind Jake to strap his wheelchair down.

"Back up a little, would you?"

Dutifully following my orders, Jake backed up. Right over my finger, which I'd foolishly left in his wheel's path.

"Yow!" I said.

"Whaaaaat happened?" Vincent asked.

I was hopping up and down shaking my hand.

"Jake ran over my finger. Holy Dinah, that smarts!"

I was overselling it. It hurt, sure, but not so bad. The tip of my left index finger was red. I crammed it into my mouth.

"I'm sorry," said Jake. "You asked me to—"

Oliver hooted. "He ran over your finger! Ran it right over, *squish!*"

Nadja said, "Should I get the school nurse?"

"Jake *says* he's sorry," I told them all, hamming it up, "but we all know what a bully he is, don't we? You ran over my finger on purpose, didn't you? Always throwing your weight around!"

Now that the kids saw I was busting Jake's chops, it became a big joke.

"Why did you run over Craig's fiiiiinger, Jake, you big bully?" Vincent asked.

"Keep your mouths shut!" Jake snapped, delighted. "There's more where that came from!"

"You see how he treats me?" I wailed. "My finger is ruined. It's my most charming feature. It's my nose-picking finger."

The kids howled. Nose picking was funny. Boogers were funny. We were proudly lowbrow. Only Nadja was unimpressed.

"Shut up!" shouted Jake. "I'll run you over—run you *all* over!"

Once the hilarity subsided I sat behind the wheel.

"Let's blow this pop stand."

I couldn't tell you when it happened, exactly. The moment when all the noticeable differences melted away and they became kids, same as any other kids. Yes, I could see the wheelchair and yes, the facial tics and yes, the florid hand gestures. But in my eyes, those things had ceased to be a definition of selfhood. They never should have defined those kids in the first place. They were just kids—*my kids*, I thought possessively. The best kids in the whole damn world.

That day's ride was a rowdy one, with at least four stories going on at the same time, everyone talking over each other.

VINCENT: Craig, do you want to hear my new stooooory?

ME: Just a sec, Vincent. Yes, Nadja?

NADJA: I am just so *angry* today.

ME: What happened?

NADJA: My friend Madison? We are at the dance class and she is getting angry at me for no reason. And now I don't want to go to sleep tonight.

ME: Why's that?

NADJA: Because Madison will be in my *dreams*.

OLIVER: Hey, guess what? Do you know that men's hearts are bigger than women's hearts?

VINCENT: Do you know some names are the same for meeen and women?

OLIVER: My name's a girl's name!

ME: *Olive* is a girl's name, not Oliver.

JAKE: What if you're a hermaphrodite?

VINCENT: Whaaaat's that?

ME: Ummm . . . a person who has both man and woman parts.

VINCENT: Like breeeasts?

ME: Yes.

VINCENT: And painted toenaaails?

ME: Well, sure. Though guys could paint their nails if they want.

OLIVER: Holy schizz! Painted toenails!

NADJA: Some names are only boy's names. Like Kevin.

JAKE: And Bruce. And Helga.

ME: And Gavin. Gavin is a manly name.

GAVIN: (*Jack LaLanne "muscleman" pose*)

OLIVER: I know a girl named Theresa. She got hit in the face with a soccer ball.

JAKE: I thought you were going to say she's a hermaphrodite.

OLIVER: Oh, yeah, she is. Also she got hit in the face with a soccer ball. I kissed her when I was in Grade 10.

ME: Oliver, you're only in Grade 8.

OLIVER: I meant Grade 6.

VINCENT: If you could give yourself a new naaame, what would it be?

NADJA: Hannah. No—*Ripley.*

JAKE: Ace.

VINCENT: I would be Biiiill. No . . . Boooob.

ME: I'd rename Oliver Damien.

OLIVER: Who's Damien?

ME: There was this movie that came out before you guys were born. *The Omen.* There was a kid named Damien. He was the son of the devil.

OLIVER: I *am* Damien! I am the son of the devil!

JAKE: Did Damien have special powers, like telekinesis?

ME: I don't remember.

NADJA: My uncle? He pushed a pop can off the table using his mind.

JAKE: I made a dollar bill twirl off the counter, once, by thinking about it.

OLIVER: I made twenty dollars vanish from my dad's wallet.

VINCENT: I can communicate with doooogs. Well, oooone dog. My own. I can tell she loooves me.

OLIVER: Hey, do you guys know this thing called, like, it's called . . . erectile dysfunction?

(*Span of silence*)

VINCENT: Craaaaig . . . ? Do you want to hear my new stooory? It's about a robot named Atomo. He was built by a Japanese farrrrmer based on blueprints found in his field in 1941. Atomo can speak all known or unknown languages, including those spoken by fiiiish.

OLIVER: I have a robot, too. His name is Norman the Butt-Kickin' Robot!

This cracked everybody up. Jake was crying, he was laughing so hard.

JAKE: What can Norman do?

OLIVER: He can rip you in half like a ten-pound phonebook. He can bend you like [*Oliver stared out the window*] like a light pole! Oh, and I hate to tell you guys this, but I just let one go.

On the bus's hierarchy of humour, perhaps the only thing funnier than nose-picking was farts. Farts trumped all, and Oliver knew how to play to his audience.

ME: You let one go? So now all of us have to smell it? Do you do that in school?

OLIVER: All the time. In my chair!

VINCENT: I guess it's true—big things come in small paaackages.

JAKE: When my mom died, my dad said he even missed the smell of her farts.

VINCENT: Jake, I'm sorry about your moooom.

NADJA: Me, too.

OLIVER: And me too.

We pulled up to a red light. A big bus idled in the next lane. The windows of both buses were wide open to let in the breeze. The kids waved back and forth, calling out greetings. Oliver asked what school the other kids went to.

"Oh, yeah," he shouted when the answer came. "My friend goes there. His name is Joey."

The light turned green. I goosed the bus up to sixty and cruised. We rolled through vibrant sunshine. Air curled through the windows, ruffling our hair. The sun hit the mirrors and spat off in sparkling radiants; its heat could be felt in the same way across the skin of each of us, that transference of light and warmth happening in all of our bodies. A glance into the riot mirror disclosed five faces turned frontward. They saw that I was smiling and they smiled back, and in that moment I understood just how lucky I was.

—

We are all the same, chemically speaking. Every living thing starts out as hydrogen: carbon and nitrogen and oxygen. These three elements emerge from a fusion process that takes place in the centre of suns. Heat splits the hydrogen into carbon, into nitrogen, into oxygen. In this way, humans are one of a trillion atomic byproducts of that intense heat. Literally, we hail from stardust.

Carbon is the chemical building block of all known life here on earth. There are a static number of carbon atoms on our planet. No more or less today than when it all started. Living things are born, they exist, they die, they break down to component elements. Those same carbon atoms go on to be part of new life. You and I are cobbled out of carbon cells that were once other things entirely. We could have a carbon cell in one of our elbows that was once part of a trilobite's tail. Or a cell from Attila the Hun's moustache in our eye. Or an ancient lotus petal in our tonsils.

Rewind the whole of human history, put the evolutionary arithmetic in reverse, and our world renders down to hydrogen: oxygen and nitrogen and carbon. Four nucleotides, too: adenine, cytosine, guanine, thymine. Every plant and animal, every insect, all of us. Any creature to have taken on life, grown, crawled, run, learned, known, felt, hoped, loved.

As those base elements networked into more complex helixes, human life diversified. Different skin colours. Different textures and colours of hair. Different shapes and hues of eyes. That diversity quickened, and glitches began to appear: A person could be born lacking the ability to walk, or smaller than average, or with conditions affecting their abilities to learn or interact. Other people could be born without a glitch but turn into humongous screw-ups despite that immense gift.

Beyond shared chemicals there is . . . I want to say "fate," if only because "luck" feels too slight. For some of the kids on my bus, the deviation is so small: an imperfection in the DNA strand so tiny that an electron microscope cranked to 100,000x magnification shows but a shadow. A knot of rogue atoms. Weightless. A body forms itself around that anomaly, and next comes a life, and the lives of that person's family.

As for Jake . . . his body became what it is for the want of a single breath of air. If his mother's lungs had continued to breathe for him—blood-borne oxygen pumped through the umbilical cord—if her blood vessels hadn't constricted, sending the carbon-dioxide concentration skyrocketing, forcing Jake's lungs to reflexively expand while still suspended in amniotic fluid . . . if he'd had just a few extra seconds (if they'd *all* had that, every kid on my bus) then Jake would have been born premature, and that would have been it. He would have grown, fleshed out, his life mapping an entirely different trajectory.

Maybe he wouldn't have moved to Canada. Why would his family have had to? And even if that move had happened for some other constellation of reasons, Jake would have numbered amongst the faceless teenage hordes filing out of the school doors every day. He might have worn a football jacket over his tall and lanky frame; he might have been a silky wide receiver with crazy-glue fingertips. He might have spotted his girlfriend waving from the practice field, her pleated cheerleader's skirt dancing around a pair of athletic legs, and his fast-twitch fibres would have triggered as he broke into a sprint to meet her—and hell, he may have darted past the bus I was driving and the two of us would have taken no reckoning of each other, both of us lacking the understanding that on a different timeline, in a different body, Jake would be in a chair strapped to the lattices running along the floor of that very bus.

How many seconds separate Jake or any of us from those burdens of fate? Three? Five? At some point in our lives, the cut may have been that fine. Who can say, and perhaps it is not worth pondering. But we do, don't we? We gnaw on that bone of possibility until our teeth are dull and our skulls throb. There are other life-lines than the one we landed on, and we can taste it.

On that bus that afternoon we followed a broken yellow line down a strip of tarmac that winnowed to a point against the horizon. We dipped into a gully and charged up a rise; the numberless suburban dwellings sprawled out below us and, many miles off, the Rocky Mountains rested in their snowcapped seats. Every eye on the bus was focused on those peaks because we are naturally drawn to such sights—and in this way, and in almost every other way, everyone on that bus was the same. We were all elementarily human.

I dropped off the kids one by one. Soon it was down to Jake and me. In the end it was always us two. We cruised the suburbs in the cooling afternoon.

"Are you driving the bus next year?"

"I don't know," I said. "Probably not."

"Okay."

"It's been great, Jake. Best job of my life."

"You want to do something else," he said simply.

What could I tell him? The truth was that this had always been a short-term gig. A springboard to other things.

I said, "I never had so much fun as I had on this bus. You know? That's pure fact."

"It was fun," Jake agreed. "I'll miss you."

"I'll miss you, too."

We lapsed into silence. The asphalt rumbled under the tires.

"I should have talked to her today."

"Maybe so. But there are worlds enough, and time." I shrugged. "I stole that line from a book."

Jake smiled. "Tomorrow is another day?"

"It is, my friend. Tomorrow is always that."

We rolled up to his house. I lowered the ramp then dashed up the driveway to ring the doorbell. We waited by the garage door under a basketball hoop nailed up by the house's prior owner. I patted Jake's chest gently.

"See you tomorrow."

"Tomorrow, tomorrow," Jake warbled, "I love ya, tomorrow. You're only a day away."

I watched him head inside the house. His caregiver gave me a wave. Back inside the bus, I hung the "EMPTY" placard in the back window and called it in.

"Craig Davidson, route 412. Checked and clear."

Here's the thing: every day was the best day, even the crappiest ones. Every single day I spent with those kids. And I was grateful, so incredibly grateful, because I knew I'd done nothing to deserve it.

16.

So rarely do things end the way we hope they will.

Last day of school. A sweltering June day: the sun beat down from a cloudless sky to broil the bus's upholstery. An unbroken stretch of school-less time loomed before my kids, tantalizingly within reach.

That final ride started benignly. After much hugging and farewells with their teachers, Gavin and Oliver hopped on board. They must've had a class party—Oliver was wired on sugar. Though not quite in Mad Scientist mode, he was on edge. He went on and on about a dumpster near his house.

"It's full of paperwork," he told me. "Like, files and forms. Some guy just threw them out!"

"And what do you do with them?"

"I fill them out."

I laughed. "Meaning . . . ?"

Oliver seemed miffed that he had to explain it any further. "I check in all the little boxes. *Duh*. Sign my name on the dotted line."

So far as I could figure, one of his neighbours had thrown out some old tax forms. "You may have a career as an accountant," I advised him.

Oliver considered this as we passed a public lake off the highway.

"Hey," he said. "My friend and I found a dead horse floating in that lake."

"You did, huh?"

"Yep. Then later, at night, we shot a tombstone."

"The horse's tombstone?"

"Yeah. Then we dug up the grave."

Jokingly, I said: "Digging up graves is illegal."

"If you called the police on me I'd hunt you down," Oliver said darkly.

The tone of his voice, the overt threat . . . it nettled me. It shouldn't have—it was just Oliver being Oliver—but it did.

"Somehow, Oliver, that doesn't scare me."

"Oh, yeah?" The Mad Scientist suddenly reared his ugly head. "I'll take a twelve-gauge shotgun, shoot it at your feet and make you dance!"

"Well, I guess I'll be waiting for you with your twelve-gauge," I said, feeling silly but still weirdly upset. "But you don't own a twelve-gauge, Oliver. Just like you didn't dig up a grave, or shoot a horse's tombstone, or find a dead horse in a lake."

Oliver goggled at me as if I was a docile dog who'd suddenly gone feral.

"I did so do all of . . . those . . . *things*!"

"You're a great storyteller. That's what you are."

Oliver said: "I'll get a BB gun and shoot you in the butt."

"You'll do what?"

"Can't you hear, dipshit?"

His voice dropped on the "shit" half of dipshit, as if in acknowledgement he'd just crossed our long-held line. I pulled over. Oliver's head was angled down. All I could see was a mass of blond locks.

"What did you just call me?"

"I didn't say anything," he mumbled.

"No, go ahead. Tell me what you said."

"Nothing, Craig. For real."

After a long stalemate I pulled back onto the road. I felt stupid and a little sick.

"If I called you a bleeping-bleep it was an accident," Oliver said.

"No, Oliver, it wasn't. If I called you a bleeping-bleep it would be on purpose. But I think you're a good guy—most days, anyway—so I don't call you names. You got to learn to own up to your actions, my friend."

I pulled up to Gavin's house. Gavin slipped silently past me and out the door. Before I could stop him, say goodbye, anything—serenading him off the bus had been the plan— he was gone.

"Gavin," I called out. "Have a great summer!"

Gavin didn't turn around. But then, he never did. Damn. I cancelled the hazard lights and pulled slowly back onto the street.

Oliver's head was still hung. "I'm sorry."

"Okay, okay, it's fine. Really. I'm sorry, too."

We pulled into the high school. My route was blocked by a fire truck. A police helicopter circled overhead. Something called "Senior Prank Day" had gotten wildly out of hand, apparently. Smoke bombs set off in the hallways, other hooliganism. My kids piled hastily on board.

"The teeeeachers couldn't stop it," said Vincent.

"Everybody is so mad," said Nadja.

"Can I go look?" asked Oliver.

We left speedily. At Nadja's stop she said goodbye to everyone—but to Jake most sweetly of all. Before stepping off she stopped in front of me. It seemed natural that something should pass between us . . . but nothing did.

"Have a great summer, Nadja."

"You too."

Vincent left the chewed stump of a pencil on his seat. He touched the nape of Jake's neck . . . then, for the first time, touched mine. Then he too was gone.

"See yooou . . ."

Next Oliver. I patted him on the shoulder—as always, telegraphing it so he could get out of the way if he chose. Oliver smiled in a melancholy way. He mumbled his goodbyes and walked up the road to his house at a slow, slump-shouldered lope.

At Jake's stop I took a moment to retrieve his water bottle, which had fallen to the floor. There was a sense—of course I can only speak for myself—that there should be something profound in our parting. An acknowledgement of how random and strange and beautiful that we'd met at this juncture in our lives.

We waited for the garage door to rise. Neither of us spoke. A warm zephyr blew down the street. Calvin came down the ramp. Smiles and handshakes.

"So," I said, "see you around, Jake my man."

"If I don't see you square." Jake's wistful smile mirrored my own. "Goodbye, Craig."

"Have a good summer. I'm sure we're gonna see each other . . ."

"Yeah. I'm sure."

"Well . . . bye."

"Yeah. Bye."

That was it. How it all ended.

One
Morning
in Time,
Revisited

From

"THE SEEKERS,"
an unpublished novel

The boy was encased in a glass tank filled with pale purple liquid. He was tall and burly, his head nearly touching the top of the tank, brown hair drifting lazily around his face. A breathing apparatus was strapped over his mouth and nose, making it difficult to tell if he was handsome—he had strong cheekbones and a sharp nose, but his eyes were closed.

He was naked. Naked as a jaybird, as old people said. Ripley felt a strange squirming in her belly. She had seen naked boys before—a boy at a foster home where she'd lived for a few months liked to walk around with no pants on—but it was different with this boy, who seemed to be sleeping inside his glass tank. It made her feel like a peeping Tom.

"This is Vincent," said Christopher.

"Put some clothes on, guy," said Oliver.

"He can't hear you, Mr. Cooke," Christopher went on. "Vincent came with . . . all this. When we found this place, we found him. He was the only living creature here."

The room where they stood was small. Other than the tank, its main feature was a control panel with many blinking lights and switches.

"We found Vincent nearly two years ago," said Christopher. "Here in this room. He hasn't moved. He is in some form of suspended animation. The Book tells us that he will release himself when everything is ready."

"What book?" said Ripley.

"Appliances and cars and even Aspirin come with instruction manuals," Christopher told her. "So does this place. But its instructions are quite a bit bigger than those in any manual. It's a Book. A rather large one, as you might imagine. In it is everything we need to keep this place running. It doesn't answer every question, but enough to put the plan into action." He held up his hand. "I know what you're going to ask. What plan? We'll get to that."

Ripley forced herself to keep her eyes trained on Vincent's face. Air bubbles came out of a vent in his facemask, following the curve of his jaw as they floated up to the—

The boy's eyes opened.

Ripley took a step back. "Has he ever done that before?"

Christopher looked at the tank. He inhaled sharply.

"No," he said, unable to hide his shock. "This is a first."

He went over to a phone on the wall. The boy in the tank

watched Ripley. His eyes an intense antifreeze blue. Was he smiling behind the mask?

"His eyes are open," Christopher told someone on the phone. "No movement, just the eyes."

When Christopher hung up, Vincent closed his eyes again. They all waited to see if he would reopen them. When it became clear he would not, Christopher said, "I have one last thing to show you."

He led them through a door on the far side of the room. Jake and Oliver tried to go through at the same time and found themselves jammed in the doorframe. Jake shot Oliver an aggravated look.

"You first, my lord," he said acidly.

"Are you trying to make me feel bad, Legs?" Oliver chuckled, stepping through the doorway in one big hop. "You don't know me very well."

The room was cramped with the five of them inside, the ceiling so low that Christopher and Gavin had to bend their knees.

Another door was set into the far wall. A tiny round door made of wood. The door had a black knob. The knob pulsed with an energy Ripley could feel over every inch of her skin—a tremor like touching a railway track as a locomotive bore down on you.

Christopher's mouth was pinched with concern—as though he, too, felt uncomfortable being so close to the door. "Step back, all of you," he said, his voice tight with strain.

He knelt and placed his hand on the doorknob. Taking a deep breath, he opened it—

Milk. That's what the substance behind the door looked like. Ripley could see its surface rippling slightly—a wall of milk. Beads of it rolled down the face of the door. What was keeping the liquid there? Why didn't it slosh out? It seemed to be moving. Rushing past the door at a swift clip. Droplets spat off the edge of the door frame and hit the floor; those drops ran back towards the door to quickly rejoin the flow.

It may have looked like milk, but Ripley knew that it couldn't be milk. Not just because it didn't behave like the stuff she'd poured on her breakfast cereal. It was more the feeling she got looking at it—the tremor became stronger, so powerful that the hairs on her arms stood up like quills.

"This," said Christopher, "is . . . time, for lack of a better word. Picture time as a stream. The current of time flows in one direction, into the future. If you want to go back, you'd have to swim against the current. It's more natural to flow with it, but it is possible to travel in the opposite direction."

Ripley looked at Oliver and Gavin. Their eyes were as wide as saucers. Jake's eyes weren't quite so big. Maybe he'd seen this before. But he was sitting bolt upright, his fingers clenched on the wheels of his chair.

"There is nothing unusual on the other side of this wall," Christopher said, indicating the wall the door was set into.

"If you were to leave this building and locate the other side of this wall, you would find yourself outside. There's a patch of grass and an anthill last I checked. But in there," he pointed to the flowing milk, "space goes on and on. We tried to measure it. We fed a long pole into it. It got swept away. Then we had a bale of rope, a thousand yards of it. We tied a weight to the end and let it spool through this door. It all went. Something snatched at it, and the rope got sucked through. The space through this door is infinite, is our best guess. As infinite as time."

"Stop it," said Oliver. His body was vibrating, but with rage or fear Ripley could not tell.

"You can move in the stream of time," Christopher went on. "You can go anywhere in history—back to before any of us were even here on earth. Or to a point when we could all be gone. All life on earth."

Oliver squeezed his eyes shut. "Stop it."

Christopher closed the door. Ripley had never been so happy to see a door shut in her life.

"It's closed, Mr. Cooke."

Oliver cracked one eyelid. He let out a shaky breath.

Nobody spoke. Ripley's mind was reeling. It couldn't be. It made no sense. Time didn't work that way. Hours and minutes and days and years weren't liquid, you couldn't see them or swim through them.

They could hear the milk—they could hear *time*—slapping rhythmically against the door. It sounded like a heartbeat.

"You say you've put poles and rope in there," said Ripley. "Have you ever put a . . ."

"A person?" Christopher shook his head. "It's incredibly dangerous to let people loose in time. Changes to the past can create terrible ripples in the present or future. So no, nobody has stepped through that door."

"Not yet," said Jake. "Isn't that what you mean?"

Christopher nodded. "Not yet."

Jake angled his chair so that he faced Ripley, Oliver, and Gavin.

He said: "So. Who wants to go swimming?"

17.

To the riders of bus 3077. The gang.

I don't know if you'll ever read this. Maybe your folks will. If so, they may tell you: "That old bus driver of yours was a bit screwed up."

Your bus driver showed up on time, acceptably dressed and clean-shaven (most days), so it was reasonable for you to assume I came to you whole. But I was slightly broken when you found me. As an adult, you must take on responsibility. But for much of my adult life until I met you, I had avoided it. I was trapped in a dream of being a writer. I didn't give a schizz about much else. The only person my isolation would really hurt was me, so who cared? That was my thinking. But my stewardship over you gave me a larger sense of accountability. Collectively, you were wonderful, magical "cargo" that somehow managed to change its carrier a little.

Remember that week when Oliver and Gavin were transferred onto Audrey's bus? There had been some kind of administrative boondoggle; I don't remember the details. But it broke up the gang. I remember driving behind Audrey's bus, and Oliver, you were in the backseat gazing out the window. You kept waving. The next day you ran over to the bus and said:

"I miss you."

It broke my heart, in the best possible sense. I'd forgotten how it felt to be necessary, even in the smallest way. The confidant. The repository of secrets and crushes and paper-smoking addictions. Big brother. Protector. Someone to be counted on. And of course I missed you and Gavin, so I badgered my boss until he switched the route back.

It was a great year. String together fifteen or twenty years like that and you could call it a pretty terrific life. At some point, driving you went from being a job to a joy. I would have done it for free. You became a needful constant in my life. If I was broken, then the bus fixed me. *You guys* fixed me. Deep inside I know that's not fair—it's a hell of a lot to ask that anyone redeem you—and yet I feel it no less keenly. The physical truth is that I drove you. The deeper truth is that you drove me. Drove me to step out of my own sickened skin, to stop feeling sorry for myself and to see the world for its beauties more than its agonies. Ultimately you drove me back to my computer with a renewed sense of purpose. For most of that year I didn't write a thing. I wasn't creatively blocked—I simply didn't think that I was any good. I could write things down, but why bother? Then, somewhere along the line, I began to feel better about myself. I was convinced I could write some of those ideas down and they wouldn't be terrible. I gained confidence; but even then, I could have stumbled—I was like a day-old foal trying to stand for the first time. I thought about the stories you told on the bus, each of you spinning your own tale. So I sat down and spun my own. I wrote a book about . . . well, *us*.

No, not *exactly* us; aspects of us. I made up names for all of you (except for Gavin)—the same names you're called in this book, in fact. You're all characters. Oddballs and castoffs with tragic histories and secrets. But you are also extraordinary—even though your powers remain unknown at first, even to yourself. It's your job to save the world. Yes, you're just kids, and a more ragtag lot would be hard to find. But everyone loves to root for the underdog, don't they?

So I began to write. I took us on an adventure. Jake always said that's what readers want: to be spirited away from day-to-day concerns and taken to a place where none of that matters. The reader says: *I wish I could be this hero or heroine—have this romance—share these friendships—kiss this girl or boy—commit this act of noble self-sacrifice—be my best self—have an experience that I could never have in real life.* I wish, I wish, I wish. And the writer tries to grant those wishes.

I called the novel "The Seekers." It sat in a desk drawer for years—until I sat down to write this book about our year together. It has been strange to leaf through those old pages again. We're all there—parts of us, anyway—suspended in time. And I like that. Time is strange and discombobulating. One day we'll wake up and there won't be any time left to do the things we always told ourselves we'd do. Time goes on and we go with it, helplessly. It's weird, because my son (yes, I have a son now) can't understand that he will get old. If he manages to avoid some of the traps that life has in store, he will grow older, become an elderly person and someday he will die. It's hard to even write that. He's only two years old right now. He can't yet understand that there will be an adolescent version of him, an adult one, and an elderly one. But his mother (yeah, I've got a wife too!) and I, we can see him changing. He's not a baby anymore. When I press my nose to the top of his head and inhale, there's still a *nice* smell, but it's not that newborn-baby-scalp smell. Since our son can't see himself getting older, I guess he can't see his mother or me or his grandparents or aunts and uncles—all the people he knows—getting older, either. To him we're all Han Solo suspended in carbonite. I don't imagine he can see the minor signs of aging that his mother and I can see in each other— and yes, even in our little boy.

That's one reason why it felt nice to flip through that old novel again. In it, we're all frozen. Unaging, unaltered, exactly the way I remember us being at that time. I feel the same way about that year we spent together. I want to keep it sacrosanct, and all of us frozen at that point on our timelines like ants in amber. Perfect in our imperfection.

What do I remember? It comes in flashes—moments, details unanchored from their connective fabric.

Gavin, I see you charging across the schoolyard to the bus, head down, arms a-pumping. Nadja, I'm remembering that list of "Bus Rules" you and I wrote out: Rule #1: Be Nice to Everybody; Rule #7: No Swears Except "Hell" and "Schizz"; Rule #22: No Farting Allowed. Vincent, I hear your stories with their bittersweet happy endings.

Oliver . . . you'd be an adult now. You could say "Holy shit" and I wouldn't be able to give you hell for it. That blows my mind. This conversation and a thousand others were so much fun:

"I'm going to call a Lamborghini dealership today. Thinking about buying one."

"They can be pricey, Oliver."

"Well, I've got a paper route."

Jake. We spoke our own language, didn't we? I could say:

"Let's stop at Yummy Yummy on the way to ferny dell with Carl the Poisoner and Jimmy Jogger, you jelly-brained gimboid!"

. . . and you'd know precisely what I'm talking about. I'm thinking about you reading that sentence right now and laughing that breathless laugh of yours, the one where you go: "Stop it, please! I'm dying!"

Your father, Calvin—a tough man himself—summed it up simply: "Jake isn't having an easy life of it." Which, okay, you're not. Yet you're somehow tougher than life. And I was such a cynic that I had to meet you to believe such toughness existed.

I remember one winter afternoon when it was minus twenty-five outside. Everybody was piled into the bus but the lift was giving me fits. And you were wearing a *tee-shirt*, Jake. You're the toughest sonofagun I've ever met, but surely not the sanest. The wind was blowing needles of snow at us and you had your eyes closed with your hair pushed back from the wind but damn it all if you weren't *smiling*. I was shivering, dumbfounded at the sheer existence of anyone so wild and vital.

—

The author Joan Didion wrote: *Writers are always selling somebody out.*

As a writer you tell yourself that you need to be accurate and tell a true story but the reality is: you were all kids in the process of becoming who you are today. Years have passed since I drove you. I suppose it might seem weird to say this— and maybe it *is* weird. But there are days when I wish we could build a machine and shuttle back through time. I'd fire up unit 3077 and drive the old route again. Pick you up and welcome you on board. The same jokes, that old familiarity. But we can't do that, I know. There's that old saying about the people you meet in life. *You can't take everyone with you.* You're probably discovering that now, if it wasn't clear before. Time gets away from us. It rips some of our friends away. People come together, they fall apart. But what I've realized, and what I hope you understand too, is this doesn't mean the memories go anywhere or are any less essential. They are more essential than ever, maybe, because you'll never build new ones with that particular group of people.

My deepest fear now is that I may have underestimated you in some critical way. I realize there's so much that I do not, and cannot, know about you. Not only about you personally, but about your possible futures. You'll run into many overly sympathetic boobs who don't expect anything exceptional from you. I don't want to be one of them. I hope to God I'm not.

Oliver, you often said that you wanted to head to Hollywood and make action movies—at least on those days when you didn't want to shack up with your girlfriend and be an electrician. I hope you do both: become an action star who does some electrical work on the side.

Nadja, I hope to see your artwork in a gallery some day.

Gavin, perhaps you are a voice-over actor—okay, okay, not that. But a small engine mechanic? Sure. I can picture that.

Vincent and Jake . . . although there are days when I wouldn't wish this on my worst enemy, you could end up as writers.

———

When people find out that I used to drive a bus for students with special needs, the common response is: "That was noble of you."

I don't bother telling them that I took the job because I was poor and nobody else would hire me. Nobility had nothing to do with it. But sometimes a person can be ennobled by circumstance.

That year taught me that none of us is perfect. Perfect body, perfect mind: the biological arithmetic stands against that possibility. I'm not even close to perfect. I have bad eyesight and prostate trouble. My son has a lazy eye and a heart murmur. Albert Einstein had Asperger's. Charles Dickens suffered from epilepsy. Tom Cruise has dyslexia. None of us is built to spec. We're all imperfect in some way, inside and out. But it's a dangerous road, aspiring to some impossible ideal of perfection. We're imperfect from the moment of conception—and so what? Those we love don't care about those imperfections, or love us more because of them.

When some people read drafts of this book, they said: "I was waiting for Gavin to speak," or "I wanted Jake to get that girl." This is a manifestation of our hopeful human nature— and of our desire for stories to have happy endings. I wish I *could* write those things. But Gavin won't speak, probably ever. Jake never did talk to that girl in social studies. These are the realities. And I have my own, far less serious realities to deal with. I likely will never be a mega-bestselling writer. I am okay with that now. I've discovered that your dreams aren't quite what you expected anyway, even if you catch a piece of them. I am a semi-successful writer. I make a living at it. Having achieved that, I can't say it's made me happy. At least not the kind of happiness I'd anticipated. Perhaps that's why people can make billions of dollars or cure diseases or entertain millions of fans and still feel depressed. Maybe they say to themselves: *I accomplished everything I set out to do, so why don't I feel the euphoria I'd expected?* But had they known how they would feel reaching the mountain peak, would they have even committed to the climb? That feeling—or that *expectancy* of feeling—is the carrot on the stick. It's the heat-shimmer on a summertime road that you chase but never catch. You don't *want* to catch it, do you? Better to chase it forever and die never reaching it.

So for me, having snatched a small piece of that dream, I can say that the joy in my life comes from the places where it had always resided. My family and friends. The woman I love. Our son. Little things, but they feel like big things. You go all the way around the horn, spending years in the wilderness, to come back to the place you always were. But at least you can appreciate it now.

Driving the bus was a small moment in the larger scope of my existence. Four hours a day, every weekday for one school year. But it could not have been bigger for me. It was *immense*.

Gavin. Vincent. Nadja. Oliver. Jake.

Every moment I spent with you was a privilege.

Thank you. I love you.

18.

My final week on the job I drove my bus out of the southern yard.

I woke to the sound of magpies cawing outside my bedroom window. I drove my rattletrap VW up Macleod Trail to the First Student impound where my bus was parked amongst others of its kind. In the yard portable I poured a cup of coffee from the carafe and dropped a dollar in the jar. Drivers milled and kibitzed. Ethel and Fran and Harry and Millicent and Hubert. Good people. By then I was one of them. I spotted a gaggle of trainees clustered round a bus, performing a pre-trip tutorial and thought: *Look at you sad, fumbling greenhorns!*

I sat at the table beside a thick-shouldered fellow named Ron, a retired NHL referee. He pulled a photograph from his wallet, working it out of its protective plastic sheath with huge squared-off fingers.

"Another grandkid," he told me. "That makes seven."

"Cute. She's going to be a heartbreaker."

"It's a boy," Ron said flatly.

"Yeah, no, I see it now. That young, it's tough to . . ."

"Chuck," Ron asked another driver. "My grandson doesn't look like a girl, does he?"

Chuck held his hand out flat, then gave it a little see-saw action. Laughter rumbled through the driver's room.

We filtered out to our buses. I cracked the hood and checked the dipstick and battery connections. Fired it up. That heady stink of diesel. I flicked on lights, hazards, performed an exterior check. Across the yard dozens of yellow-vested drivers pre-tripped their own buses. All over the world thousands of drivers would be doing the same that day. In Japan and England, Russia and Italy, Mexico, Spain, France, Timbuktu. Anywhere there were children and schools and roads that separate them. The buses were yellow in North America— the colour is actually called *School Bus Yellow*—green in El Salvador, orange in Honduras, white in Ireland, blue in the Netherlands, red in Nicaragua. They would be driven by men and women named Hector, Boris, Masahiru, Ikbar, Graciela. That morning we would transport tens of millions.

I joined the convoy of buses heading out of the yard. The sun elevated into its eastern altar. Squirrels dashed across the fence, bodies coiling through the metal links. Buses exited the yard as a stately yellow flotilla, dispersing into the urban grid. A smaller number of smaller buses lacking no smaller agenda broke off from the fleet. Channel one on your CB radio, number one in your hearts.

And the radio was jumping that morning. A couple Code Yellows, three driver no-shows, traffic snarls all over the map. Oooh, boy. The poor souls in the dispatcher's office were probably popping Advils like Tic Tacs.

First stop: Jake. What would we talk about? The usual, probably. And hey, the usual was always good. Next Vincent. Double back for Oliver. Nadja. Gavin. I hoped nobody was sick. We were all happiest when everybody was riding. The whole crew, whole cloth. To the west over the mountains the sky darkened with rain, but my mood was light.

This was how it would happen:

I'd pull up. The ramp would lower. The door would open. They'd clamber aboard in Converse high-tops and snow-boots and a Pronto M94 Power Wheelchair. In hockey jerseys, unbelted trousers and skinny jeans. They would come with comic books, chewing gum, drawings of princesses and cyborgs, iPods, skateboards, loose-leaf binders, video games, teeth-bitten pencils, cough drops, lunchboxes, and hackey sacks. Jake would come with his cellphone on a lanyard. Oliver with a cellphone photo of himself beside a yellow sports car he had bought for a hundred bucks. Vincent with his newest story curled in his fist like an elder's scroll. Nadja with a back-pack heavy as a cinderblock. Gavin would come smelling of fabric softener and smell the same when the day was done. They would come with their adult spectrum meds: Valium,

Prozac, Tegretol, Seroquel. Jake would come with neurotoxic protein shot through his hips. All would come with their scars. They would come with their hopeful truths. With all the butt kickin' robots, rebelling hookers, shockingly fecund women with nine thousand husbands, telepathic dogs and telekinetic schoolboys, Thunder and Gus, Ace and Damien and Joey, hapless injury-prone in-laws, hockey-mask-wearing lesbian immortals, musclemen and scarecrows, vampires who turn into electric guitars for some reason, werewolves and shape-shifters and janitors with heat-ray vision. Jake would come with lingering pressure on his skin where Calvin had pressed their foreheads together, as he did each morning.

Positive. Stay positive.

Perhaps they would remember little of this bus or their experience on it. In the mornings they often boarded tired or listless; in the afternoons they could be cranky or with-drawn. They rode because their parents told them to and they obeyed. But, I thought: the odd moment may persist.

Maybe it would be that afternoon in January when I had to get the bus inspected, which made me late. Darkness was falling by the time everyone was on board. A flash squall touched down. Snow curled over the Rockies on a bone-searching wind that screamed through seams in the airframe, rocking the bus on its axles. We charted a path on roads frozen to black glass. Snowflakes glittered in the headlights like a million airborne razor blades. I'd merged with a rural highway on the city's southernmost scrim. The glow of car headlights pooled up and across the night rises. The moisture of six bodies fogged the windshield; I'd rolled down the window and wind howled with such force that the tears forced out of my eyes were vaporized before they touched my ears. The tires lost traction on a strip of black ice and hit the rumble strips before returning to the tarmac. My fists were gripped fierce to the wheel—which was when Jake began to sing.

It's cold outside, there's no kind of atmosphere
I'm all alone, more or less . . .

Darkness wrapped tight to the bus, snow pelted the windows, and Jake belted out the theme song to *Red Dwarf* in a high clear British-accented contralto.

. . . Let me fly, far away from here
Fun, fun, fun, in the sun, sun, sun . . .

Such are the memories I would take away. The memories I'd die holding, I sincerely hoped. Six souls in a bus. Nearly one-billionth of our planet's skyrocketing population. Pressed together by circumstance and necessity. But it worked. My God, it *worked*.

At the end of that last week in June I would drop my kids off for the final time. Clip the "EMPTY" sign in the window. I would drive to the summer storage yard and park this bus nose-to-tail with dozens of its kind. The half-dozen paper-backs I'd read over the months while waiting for the school bell to ring would be emptied out of the glovebox into a plastic grocery sack. Beneath them I would discover a drawing Nadja had given me the previous September. A princess in a pink gown. This I would fold gently and slip into my pocket.

For the final time I would radio it in: "Route 412, checked and clear." I would set the bus alarm, close the doors and lock them. Next year the unit would be assigned to another driver, who would pick up different kids. The bus would not remember us. Metal possesses no memory; my bus was but a shell and it would be cleansed of the personality we'd bequeathed it. But I'd always remember. I would walk out of that storage yard with the knowledge that I cannot offer a perfect ending—but stories, like the lives they chronicle, are seldom tied up with a lovely red bow. We are all imperfect, aren't we, if not by birth then eventually by age and circumstance and, if anything, that fallibility makes those who love us already love us even more deeply.

There can be no true end to a story like this. It's a story about life, which is to say it just keeps on going—as it does right now, this minute, as I write these words; and as it does when you read them. But each life is made up of many stories. That's my belief. Stories inside stories like a Russian doll. Those that come earlier serve to inform those still to come. You carry those stories and the people who shaped them forward

with you, close to your heart. And so this story, this year, cul-
minates as so much of life does: unresolved and bittersweet.
Not entirely happily, yet not without its earned measure of joy.

———

The final morning I made a right turn and passed through
an intersection, made another right and hit a clean stretch of
asphalt. I gave the bus some gas to merge in front of the cars
accelerating off a green light behind me. The *ticka-tick*ing
engine sent a shiver through the steering wheel. I goosed the
odometer up to eighty and tacked the needle, just like my
instructor Don had taught me to do all those months ago.

If you want to be rich, be rich.

Sing it, Don. Preach on.

Now finally, dear reader, let me ask you the smallest of
favours.

If today is a school day, you'll probably spot a cheese wagon.
You will see children in its windows. If you can, make a little
room. It can be one hell of a rowdy ordeal piloting these
beastly big rigs.

And hey—we're not transporting potatoes here, people!

We pass through your existence bearing precious cargo.

From
"THE SEEKERS,"
an unpublished novel

So. Who wants to go swimming?

Ripley lay on her bed in her room at the compound considering Jake's words, the ones he had spoken over two weeks ago now.

The last fourteen days had blown her mind. The things she had learned, the new shape her life was taking—it felt like make believe. Still, she wanted to quit most days. Jake barely spoke two words to her. And Oliver! That guy was genetically engineered to get on her nerves. Gavin kicked ass on every challenge Christopher threw at them without breaking a sweat. That ticked her off. She was scraping and clawing. But she was getting better.

Christopher had given them all names—ones pulled from the Book. Gavin was Goshawk. Vincent was Panther. Jake was Kodiak. Oliver was Lamprey.

"An eel?" Oliver said when Christopher told him what a

lamprey was. "Why do I have to be the eel? Why can't I be the Kodiak?"

"You'll accept the name you've been given, Mr. Cooke," said Christopher.

"How can he be a bear?" Oliver said, pointing at Jake. "He can't even walk!"

Ripley's name was Bloodhound. She had to admit there was something cool about it. A badge of membership. It had been so long since she'd belonged to something. A tribe—even if she didn't get along with her fellow tribespeople.

She lay on the bed staring at the ceiling. The spider appeared. Its legs pushed out of its hole, its body following. It crept a few inches down the wall and stopped as if waiting for her to speak.

"Hello, little buddy."

She wondered if Christopher knew about the spider. She suspected he did—he knew almost everything, even if he didn't always share that information.

Would she go? She had asked herself this a million times. When that little wooden door opened, could she slip into the Milk? Into time? She could die in there . . . and worse. You could get lost in time, Jake said. If you missed your exit door, time would sweep you away like a leaf in a fast-running river. You could get older and older but never quite die. You could live a billion years in the Milk, older than any human being should ever live. That much pure time would drive you mad.

Why her? She'd asked herself that a million times, too. Why any of them? A shrimp. A mute. A kid in a wheelchair. A kid in a glass tank. And her. A bunch of losers, just like Oliver said. Misfit toys. Factory recalls. Weren't there a billion better specimens? Smarter, more athletic kids? Ones who came from good families and weren't colossal screwups? Maybe not. Like Christopher said, they were the ones who had appeared on the list. Somehow, they were meant to do this.

"What do you think, spider? Should I go?"

The spider did not move. Ripley had the strangest feeling it was watching her.

She had the chance to do something nobody on earth had ever done. People had gone into space and down to the bottom of the sea but nobody had ever taken a trip into time. And isn't that what life was about? An opportunity to really *be* something?

Where does the time go?

She could find out, couldn't she? She had the chance to enter time itself. To see where it went. And it would be terrifying, sure, and it would ask everything of her—of all of them—and they might never know comfort or true safety again . . . but who else had been given a chance to take such a grand adventure—maybe the greatest one of all?

The door opened. Christopher stood there looking grave and slightly panicked.

"We have to go, Ms. Ripley. Right *now*. Will you come?"

Ripley sat up on the bed. The spider was gone, back in its hole.

Christopher held the door open. Ripley could see a nerve ticking excitedly down his neck. The sound of an alarm bell pealed somewhere down the hallway.

"Time, Ms. Ripley, is of the essence. So, here we find ourselves. I cannot ask again. Are you coming?"

It all came down to this. But isn't that how all lives go? Our existence boils down to a few crucial moments—and the choices we make when those moments arrive.

Ripley stood up.

"Yes," she said.

And then, more assertively: "*Yes.*"

Ladies and gentlemen—Bus Elvis!

ACKNOWLEDGEMENTS

First, thanks to my agent, Kirby Kim. He's not only a tireless, dogged supporter of my work, he's a good friend. I owe him a lot. He picked me up off the slagheap and helped me get into the game again. The fact that you're even holding this book now is, in great part, because of his unflagging efforts.

Second, thanks to my editor, Lynn Henry. I could sing Lynn's praises forever, until she got sick of hearing them—*Enough, Craig, for God's sake!*—so I will simply say that Lynn took the rough and untidy elements of the first draft of this book and, with keen sensitivity and a delicate hand, helped turn it into something immeasurably better. She has performed this subtle magic trick many times before, with me and other writers, but I'm especially grateful for her work on this manuscript.

I'd like to thank First Student for hiring me, Don and others for training me, and my fellow drivers for passing the time of day with me.

Big thanks to Kathe Lemon at *Avenue* magazine, who published the original article, "Precious Cargo," that led to me writing this, the expanded version.

Thanks to Dr. Chris Young, Dr. Michael Fehlings and Dr. Darcy Fehlings for opening their labs to me. The initial draft of this book included chapters detailing visits to those labs, and the remarkable work these doctors are doing on behalf of children with special needs; although ultimately it was decided that those chapters (however compelling) might take readers out of the on-the-bus narrative, I am deeply grateful to these doctors for taking the time. They and thousands of other physicians around the world are doing wonderful, life-changing work, and they have my highest admiration.

Thank you to my wife Colleen for simply being there— through the rough times, especially. Got to taste the bitter to appreciate the sweet. I'm so fortunate to have you there through it all, baby.

Thanks to our son, Nick, for just being him. That's all a three-year-old can really *be*—elementally and essentially himself. You sure do make life interesting, kiddo.

My greatest thanks go to the kids on bus 3077 and their parents. Honest to goodness, I didn't *write* this book as much as write it *down*. Anytime those kids said something hilarious or quizzical or profane or insightful or humane—well, I'd rush to my notebook (not while actively driving!) and jot it down. All the best lines in this book were gifted to me. But with that gift comes a burden, and it's one that will forever

be my concern. The kids in this book are not fictional characters—the type I have trafficked in most of my career. I
hope that I approached both the writing and lead-up to the
publication of this book in a correct and fair way. I realize
what an immense blessing my experience on the bus was, and
my dearest wish is to have handled everything with honesty,
tenderness, and empathy.

So thank you, finally and most crucially, to Nadja, Vincent,
Gavin, Oliver, and Jake.

Craig Davidson was born in Toronto and grew up in St. Catharines, Ontario. He has published four books of literary fiction, including *Rust and Bone*, which was made into a Golden Globe-nominated film of the same name, and *Cataract City*, which was shortlisted for the Scotiabank Giller Prize and the Trillium Book Prize, was a national bestseller, and has been optioned for film. He has also published bestselling thrillers and horror novels under the pseudonym Nick Cutter. Craig Davidson lives in Toronto with his wife and son.